# TRANSFORMING POWER FOR PEACE

Reprinted 1986

*Lawrence S. Apsey*

*James Bristol*

*Karen Eppler*

Alternatives to Violence Project
15 Rutherford Place, New York, NY 10003
and
Friends General Conference

# ACKNOWLEDGEMENTS

In updating the text for the Revision of 1964, I was extremely grateful for the assistance of James E. Bristol in preparing the "Epilogue to Chapter 7", which has become Chapter 8 in the current revision. In this revision, I wish to acknowledge the invaluable assistance of Karen Eppler, who has brought the text up to date, revised the Suggested Reading sections and written the new Chapter 12  on Transforming Power in the Labor Movement. Thanks are due also to Abby Hadley, for the final paste-up, and to Lynne Shivers, for the final proofreading. The 1981 Revision would not have been made without the help of these three.

Lawrence S. Apsey

# FOREWORD

FOR THE FIRST TIME in history, man is forced to choose between the institution of war and the continuation of the earth as a fit place in which to live. There can, of course, be only one intelligent choice; yet most people seem still to admit the possibility, if not even the probability, of nuclear and germ warfare. The reluctance to make the intelligent choice seems to stem from the belief that we must take the lesser of two evils: either nuclear and germ warfare or the violent imposition upon us of a system against our conscience. There is, however, a constantly increasing fund of experience which demonstrates that the just rights of people may be preserved without resort to violence.

The only argument which can be made against reliance on this experience is that it will not work in the current crisis, because conditions are different from those in which it has been successfully applied. It is said that not enough people understand non-violent methods or have the patience to learn, or the courage to apply them. This is a counsel of defeat which is wholly inconsistent with the faith, behavior and testimony of Friends. If members of the Society believe that alternatives to war exist, now is the time to study and master the well proven techniques of non-violence and by powerful action to lay them on the conscience of the world. The tragic crisis of the race calls everyone to dedicate some part of his life to the understanding, improvement and propagation of these techniques.

# TABLE OF CONTENTS

# 1 | TRANSFORMING POWER— ALTERNATIVE TO MASS DESTRUCTION

*To be or not to be, that is the question.*—Shakespeare

THE WORLD is waiting to be shown how the right can be upheld without violence. Mere abstention from violence has failed to uphold it; but there is a power which has proved itself capable of transforming evil situations into good ones without violence. When properly understood and applied, it has brought about great advances in human freedom. Gandhi called this power "Satyagraha," which means "adherence to truth,"[1] and many know it by the term "non-violence"; but since its objective is not to suppress an evil situation but to transform it into a good one, we shall frequently refer to it as "Transforming Power." By this term we mean to include all techniques for resolving conflicts by the persistent communication of "conscientious concerns" through loving and non-violent action. It involves a readiness to modify one's beliefs as further light may indicate; but until so modified, one must be prepared to suffer every sacrifice to maintain them without violence.

The use of this power is not limited to those who profess to be religious or to follow any particular faith. It is freely available to all who are willing to express the potential love and courage which are part of life itself. The world may well undertake the serious study and propagation of this power, which history has shown to be the key to peace and justice for all people.

The renunciation of violence is the first step to an understanding of Transforming Power. Many religious groups have taken

1

this step. Buddhists were among the first. Bahais, Mennonites and the Church of the Brethren have long made a strong and constant witness against violence. The Society of Friends did so 300 years ago when its leaders made the following declaration to Charles II.

"We utterly deny all outward wars and strife, and fightings with outward weapons, for any end, or under any pretense whatever; this is our testimony to the whole world. The spirit of Christ by which we are guided is not changeable, so as once to command us from a thing as evil and again to move us unto it; and we certainly know and testify to the world, that the spirit of Christ, which leads us into all Truth, will never move us to fight and war against any man with outward weapons, neither for the kingdom of Christ nor for the kingdoms of this world. . . . Therefore, we cannot learn war anymore."

This statement alone, however, did not make the Society a vital force for peace. But when it was put into practice by William Penn and his colonists in their dealings with the Indians, it became effective. "For . . . [seventy[2]] years the Quakers lived in absolute peace. Others were slain, others were massacred, others were murdered, but the Quakers were safe. Not a Quaker woman suffered assault, not a Quaker child was slain, not a Quaker man was tortured, and when at last under pressure, the Quakers gave up the government of the colony and war broke out, only three Quakers were killed and these had so far fallen from their faith as to carry weapons of defense. . . . The Indians did not recognize those to be Quakers who carried guns to shoot at other people.[3]"

In modern times, few Friends have an opportunity to found colonies amongst potentially hostile people and to demonstrate the power of their peace testimony on a grand scale as did the followers of William Penn. Being thinly spread among millions who support the principle of deterrence through violence, many

2

Friends fail to take positive action to advance the peace testimony and are content with a purely negative witness against war. This attitude has little effect on public opinion because it fails to grapple with the issues which are moving others to violence. It tends to give the false impression that the consciences of Friends are limited to a protest against war and that they have little concern for the freedom of people to choose their own government, to speak their minds openly or even to be protected from rape or murder at the hands of an enemy. This wrong impression is counteracted, to some extent, by those Friends who have acted positively in support of the issues of conscience which concern non-Friends as well.

If refugees from Vietnam, Cambodia or Palestine are starving, we rush to help and pour out our treasure to relieve the suffering. If victims of atomic bombing come to our shores, we open our homes and hearts to receive them. But when we are told that in the first strike of a nuclear war there will be 253 million casualties in the United States and Soviet Union,[4] that this single attack will kill more people than all of the wars prior to World War II combined, that many cities of all combatant countries will be reduced to rubble, and that the radioactive fallout will contaminate the entire world and result in defective babies for countless generations, we do little about it. In common with others, we are stunned by this information and we find difficulty in accepting it as realistic. The magnitude of the problem tends to make us evade the issue by losing ourselves in lesser problems. We have the love which would do anything to prevent such a result, but many of us do not accept the reality that it may occur or do not have faith in the power of the spirit in men's hearts to overcome it. Yet, if the day ever comes when some few of us survive such an attack and are faced with the task of rebuilding life in an incinerated world of corpses and anguished survivors, the remorse of having failed to go all out to prevent this occurrence will be unbearable.

We cannot assume that the Spirit which sustained the martyrs in the Roman arena and the Friends who were hanged for their protests against religious intolerance is dead. It can also move the people of our day and prove as invincible as in the past. But it can work only through the hearts and deeds of individuals. Its power lies in the weight of the concern which we permit it to lay upon us. The lengths to which we will go in action and sacrifice are evidences of the weight of the concern. Mankind has never faced a concern as weighty as this one. As Friends, are we ready to act on it by putting our beliefs into practice?

## Topics for Discussion

1. What methods of loving communication can you think of which might be successful in reconciling conflicts?

2. Why has it been said that a tyrant cannot long remain in power without the support of his people?

3. What can we do to be filled with the power of the Spirit which gave early Christians and Friends the ability to transform evil into good without violence?

4. What is the difference between a negative and a positive peace testimony?

5. What considerations tend to arouse in us today a concern for the study and practice of the power to transform others without violence?

## Suggested Reading

Leo Tolstoy, *Kingdom of God and Peace Essays* (Oxford University Press, 417 Fifth Ave., New York, N. Y., 1946).

Elizabeth Janet Gray, *Penn* (Viking Press, New York, 1938, $4.00).

Robert C. Aldridge, *The Counterforce Syndrome: A Guide to U.S. Nuclear Weapons and Strategic Doctrine* (Institute for Policy Studies, 1901 Q Street, N.W., Washington D.C., 1979).

Sidney Lens, *The Day Before Doomsday: An Anatomy of the Nuclear Arms Race* (Beacon Press, New York, N.Y., 1978).

Dr. Helen Caldicott, *Nuclear Madness* (Autumn Press, Boston, Ma., 1979). *The Effects of Nuclear War,* Congress of the United States, Office of Technological Assessment, 1979 (Obtainable from the Superintendent of Documents, U.S. Government Printing Office, Washington, D.C. 20402).

# 2 | TRANSFORMING ACTION AS A WAY OF LIFE

*I lived in the virtue of that life and power that took away the occasion of all wars.*—George Fox.

*No man is an ilande.*—John Donne.

IT IS A STRANGE PHENOMENON that groups which become great movements through the practice of obedience to the Spirit lose much of their effectiveness once they achieve initial success. Christianity resorted to violence, the Indian Congress Party now accepts violence as a practical necessity, and the Society of Friends no longer operates with the faith which moved its founders to history-changing acts. Each group lost its Transforming Power because it ceased fully to practice its beliefs. Be it said to the credit of the Society of Friends and the other peace churches that they have not approved the use of violence. Hence, they are in a position to demonstrate the power of love with greater influence than those who support nuclear deterrents. For this reason they bear a heavy responsibility to prove that love can overcome evil through Transforming Power. To do this, active love and truth must become a way of life; and this means that we must first understand what is required of us and then practice it daily until it is second nature.

We build active love and truth into our daily lives by consistently cultivating certain attitudes of mind, which will now be discussed.

*Identification With All Humanity.* Psychology has discovered that successful therapy toward disturbed people requires the nurse to relate herself to the patient, if only by sitting next to

5

him at first, until he is gradually drawn out of himself.[1] The nurse does this because she is concerned for the patient and wants to help. We can cultivate the same attitude toward those with whom we differ. If we reverence their potential, we can break down the barriers which prevent us and them from influencing each other. Are we willing to learn, like the nurse, to relate ourselves sympathetically to those of whose actions we disapprove—militarists, bigots, materialists, delinquents, and those whose race, religion or ideology differ from our own? Until we do this, their minds are closed to us. This is the method of those early Friends who acted in the faith that there is "that of God in every man."

*Achieving a "Sense of the Meeting" With Others.* Friends have long conducted their meetings for business by permitting the sincere views of each individual to mingle until a "sense of the meeting" is achieved. Ideas are advanced only tentatively until they have been exposed to the full impact of all conscientious differences. Great care is taken not to submerge the convictions of any individual; and if conscientious differences cannot be reconciled, action is postponed. We should practice this method as the first approach to every difference, with the aim in mind of achieving a "sense of the meeting" with all of our associates and adversaries.

With this aim uppermost, we shall avoid the fatal tactics based on the desire to get the better of our adversaries. We shall not try to prove our superiority or their inferiority; and we certainly shall not try to humiliate or frighten them or threaten them with dire results or physical harm. Our first efforts will be to put our adversaries at ease, to convince them that they have nothing to fear from us and no good reason to be hostile. This brings them nearer to the point at which they can examine the issues sincerely and dispassionately. The best way to put them at ease is by words and acts which indicate that we love them and wish them well; and the best way to find such words and acts is to feel love towards them. This is why Jesus told us to love our enemies. We must recognize that sometimes

6

the most violent party to a dispute is not our adversary, but ourselves. We must, therefore, diligently search for our own subconscious resentments, in order that we may dissipate them by realizing how totally they are defeating our true objectives. It is not as hard as it sounds, if we adopt the attitude of the nurse trying to relate herself to the disturbed patient. It took courage for Penn and his followers to approach the Indians unarmed. It took love to pay them for their land and to perform acts of mercy to those who needed help. But it worked. The Indians lost their fear and hostility.

*Re-examining and Adjusting to the Facts.* When our adversaries are sincere, their fear or hostility may be based on a different understanding of the facts. A loving attitude will not be enough to remove this difference. We must recognize at once that *we* may be mistaken as to the facts or may be drawing the wrong conclusion from them. In such event, we must quickly and gracefully change our position, for readiness of one party to adjust to new facts and arguments hastens adjustment by the others—as all who have sat at a bargaining table will testify. Extended discussion and research may be all that is required to achieve a "sense of the meeting." Patience in a joint search will usually uncover the truth. A careful exchange of facts will disclose flaws in reasoning. If facts or reasoning cannot be reconciled, a willingness to compromise on a sensible course will follow, if the parties are sincere.

*Standing Firm When Reason Fails.* We shall be fortunate indeed if love and adjustment to the facts alone achieve a "sense of the meeting." Adversaries do not often yield to love and reason if they have deep prejudices or strong selfish motives. At this point, firmness has to *force* them to adopt a fair and unprejudiced attitude. This is never done by violence, but experience has shown that the force of a just cause, long persisted in, actually dissolves prejudice and selfishness. Several factors combine to convince the adversary that unfair and selfish actions do not pay. He is firmly and continuously frustrated in his attempts to accomplish his ends; his opponent is suffering courageously and maintaining his good will; and, as a result, the bystanders are sympathizing with his opponent and disapproving of his action. This unexpected and unfavorable turn of events leads him to reconsider his motives. Seeing his fine plans go awry, he begins to question the soundness of his methods. He begins to wonder whether there may not be merit in beliefs for which his opponent so willingly suffers. It may dawn on him that he could accomplish much more by enlisting the cooperation of those whom he has been trying to dominate. He may at last even see how prejudiced, unfair and selfish he has been. The history of Gandhi's movements in South Africa and India is an example of this process at work in the minds of one after another of the officials and statesmen with whom he had to deal. Finally it had its effects on the British public and Government.

Some have objected to the use of *all* force, non-violent as well as violent, on the ground that there is no distinction in principle between the two. There is, however, a great difference, not only in degree and destructiveness, but also in moral principle. Non-violence gradually dissolves prejudice and selfishness while violence only suppresses them in such a way that they will rise again with redoubled fury when opportunity permits. As we shall see, the early Christians and Friends, as well as the followers of Gandhi, never hesitated to use non-violent force against bigotry or tyranny.[2] Indeed, force is unavoidable in every conflict based on prejudice or selfishness. One party or the other will use it and the only question is whether the victim will submit or attempt to overcome selfish force with soul force. For example, Bayard Rustin has pointed out that by sitting beside a prejudiced white person at table, a black person may apply great force against the white person—even to the point of making him physically ill in some cases. On the other hand, the white person who insists that blacks be segregated at meals is also applying force—a force which deprives the black of his self-respect and status as another human being. This is a prejudiced and degrading force. If reason fails to overcome it, should it be

8

perpetuated by a squeamishness against the use of moral force to remove it? Admittedly, it will take prolonged persistence and much suffering and discord to accomplish this; but unless reasonable people have the courage to confront this prejudice squarely and forcibly with the truth, it could continue for 3,000 years. This is what happened to the untouchables of India before Gandhi applied Satyagraha against untouchability.[3]

Of course, one does not go around applying moral force to everyone with whom one disagrees. Considerate goodwill, lengthy discussion and adjustment of viewpoints are thoroughly tried out before non-violent force is even thought of. The prejudiced white person is considerately asked if the black may sit beside him at table. If he objects, it is explained that the individual black is friendly and socially acceptable in every way and that the color of his skin is an unreasonable basis for discrimination. Only after this approach has failed, would an attempt be made to seat the black over the objection of the white person.

The firmness must always be greater and more prolonged than the selfishness or prejudice of an adversary. When a position is taken against a strong and violent adversary, it will be necessary to be as firm as a rock, fully prepared to suffer any consequence rather than yield to evil. Gandhi felt so strongly on this point that he deemed it better to resort to violence than to yield a concern of conscience because of inability to pursue the firmness and sacrifice of Satyagraha.[4] At the same time, one must be quite prepared to yield on minor points.

*Faith in the Power of Truth.* Firmness, like that displayed by the early Christians and Friends and followers of Gandhi, is impossible in the presence of fear or doubt. It comes only from faith—the deep conviction that the position for which one stands is part of the eternal truth; that being true, it will survive and can be brought into expression by those who will uphold it at all cost. It must be a truth prized more highly than security, reputation, or, in extreme cases, even life itself. This is why we have said that Transforming Power is directly

9

proportional to the weight of the concern. Gandhi thought it was the most powerful tool of man—much more powerful than violence in any form. This is true because it spreads from person to person, never surrenders and survives all fallacies.

This faith arises from communion with the universal intelligence back of life itself. Science clearly reveals that life is greater than ourselves and seeks to perpetuate itself for reasons beyond our ken. Regardless of our religion, or lack of it, we can have complete confidence that if we support the laws of harmonious living, the life which we are thus perpetuating will support our effort.

Groups which have used spiritual power to change history have had different ways of achieving this faith. To the early Christians and Friends and the followers of Dr. Martin Luther King, it came from the love of Christ; to Gandhi it came from a belief that God is Truth. The particular symbols are unimportant, but a belief in a sustaining life beyond ourselves is essential. Yet belief is not enough. Users of spiritual power have turned constantly to this life for inspiration and strength. Prayer was the mainstay of early Christians. Friends had their meetings for silent worship. Gandhi had prayers every day and practiced one day of silence each week. When it was time for prayers, he would desert even the most important political conference. Maintaining a continuous flow of inspiration and power was paramount to him. The blacks protesting segregation on the buses in Montgomery had their mass prayer meetings once a week;[5] and periods of group soul-searching preceded and accompanied the demonstrations against nuclear testing in Nevada,[6] the voyage of the *Golden Rule* in protest against nuclear testing, the disarmament rally at the United Nations, all of the United Farm Worker strikes and the vigil against germ warfare at Fort Detrick, Maryland. The weight of our common concerns as Friends must, as in the past, come out of our personal devotions and our meetings for worship, for it is only in the constant nurturing of the spiritual life that we can experience the tenderness, the courage and the faith to make Transforming Power a way of life to overcome evil.

10

## Topics for Discussion

1. Is it enough to believe in the power of love? If not, what more is necessary?

2. Discuss various methods by which we can begin to feel at one with people with whom we disagree.

3. How are differences resolved in Friends' business meetings? At the bargaining table?

4. What is required to reach agreement with people who are so prejudiced or selfish that they are not interested in reason or truth?

5. How do we achieve the power to suffer and sacrifice rather than yield to evil?

## Suggested Reading

Richard B. Gregg, *The Power of Nonviolence* (Schoken Books, New York, N.Y., 1966).

Mohandas K. Gandhi, *Collected Works* (International Publications Service).

Martin Oppenheimer and George Lakey, *A Manual for Direct Action* (Quadrangle Books, Chicago, Ill., 1965).

Erich Fromm, *The Art of Loving* (Harper & Bros., 1956).

# 3 | HOW TRANSFORMING POWER HAS BEEN USED IN THE PAST— BY EARLY CHRISTIANS

PERHAPS THE MOST FREQUENT argument against Transforming Power as a practical solution of current conflicts is that it will not work against a godless dictatorship or a pagan nation. Gandhi's success against a Christian nation with a strong moral conscience is said to be no indication that similar methods could prevail against a nation like Communist China, the Soviet Union, or South Africa.

This argument ignores the lessons of history. The Roman Empire during the first three centuries of Christianity equaled modern dictatorships in ruthlessness, paganism and violence. Nevertheless, during this period, Christianity, by its witness of love and sacrifice, grew from a tiny Jewish sect to become a religion professed by the majority in the most populous areas of mankind.[1] In the words of K. S. Latourette, a leading historian of the period, "Never in so short a time has any other religious faith or, for that matter, any other set of ideas, religious, political or economic, without the aid of physical force or of social or cultural prestige, achieved so commanding a position in such an important culture."[2]

During this period, Christians refused service in the army;[3] and there is no direct evidence that they ever used force against the bloodthirsty persecutions to which they were subjected.[4] While paying lip service to the mythology of the ancients, most people in the Empire at the time of Jesus recognized no responsibility to a divine power beyond themselves and their rulers spared no cruelty in the ten major persecutions which were launched against the Christians. Under Nero, Christians were torn by dogs or nailed to crosses and set on fire to serve at night

12

as living torches.[5] Under Valerian, the death penalty was enforced for meeting in church and entering cemeteries. Christian leaders were exiled for not doing homage to the pagan gods. Clerics were put to death, others deprived of property, enslaved or burned at the stake.[6] Christians were happy, without resistance by force, to share the martyrdom of Jesus;[7] and this had a tremendous effect in converting those who witnessed their suffering.[8] The Christians disregarded the restrictive laws and continued to witness to the power of the Spirit regardless of the consequences. The truth, as they saw it, was much more precious than life; and they never ceased to act publicly and privately in proclaiming their beliefs.

At last, even the Emperor was converted. He had a waking vision of a cross bearing the inscription "Conquer by this"[9] and it is one of the greatest tragedies of history that he was unable to interpret this vision in the light of the teachings of Jesus. Had he been sensitive to the tenderness of the divine love, Constantine would have understood his vision to mean that he should conquer by love, courage and self-sacrifice (Transforming Power) even as the Christians had conquered his Empire. Instead, he interpreted it as a guarantee of victory by the same violence that had failed against the Christians—provided only that he would profess Christianity and adopt the cross as his symbol. This was a prostitution of the message of Jesus and a prelude to centuries of the propagation of Christianity by the sword. It is small wonder that today non-Christians conceive of Christianity as one of the most bloodthirsty of religions. Not only is Constantine's interpretation of his vision accountable for the propagation of Christianity by the sword which resulted in the Crusades of the Middle Ages; but in our day the so-called Christian nations have, in the name of Christ, engaged in wars of unprecedented cruelty, destroying combatants and non-combatants alike, until at the present moment they are preparing for an Armageddon which threatens to make the world unfit for habitation.

Behind this Armageddon, is there a possibility of the Millennium, the establishment of the Kingdom of Peace? Can we recapture the power of love-witnessing by which Christianity conquered the Roman world without violence?

Modern Transforming Power, it is argued, cannot accomplish the results of early Christianity because it is not a religion. If faith and practice in the teachings of Jesus, the Apostles and the Ten Commandments is a religion, however, then Transforming Power is a religion, for its basic principles are the same. Is it religion to believe that as children of a divine Father we are all brothers and sisters, to love our neighbors as ourselves? Here are the principles we are discussing embedded in the teachings of the New Testament:

"You have heard that it was said to the men of old, 'you shall not kill; and whoever kills, shall be liable to judgment.' But I say to you that everyone who is angry with his brother shall be liable to judgment; whoever insults his brother shall be liable to the council, and whoever says 'you fool!' shall be liable to the hell of fire."[10]

"All who take the sword will perish by the sword."[11]

"You have heard it said, 'An eye for an eye and a tooth for a tooth.' But I say to you, Do not resist one who is evil. But if anyone strike you on the right cheek, turn to him the other also and if anyone would sue you and take your coat, let him have your cloak as well; and if anyone force you to go one mile, go with him two miles."[12]

"You have heard that it was said, 'You shall love your neighbor and hate your enemy.' But, I say to you, love your enemies and pray for those who persecute you."[13]

"If your enemy is hungry, feed him; if he is thirsty, give him drink; for by so doing you will heap burning coals on his head. Do not be overcome by evil, but overcome evil with good."[14]

This is Transforming Power and while it was practiced by most Christians it was the power of Christianity. In its revival lies the greatest hope of overcoming the threat of universal destruction and of establishing a just and lasting peace.

## Topics for Discussion

1. How does history indicate that ruthless people, committed to violence, who do not believe in God, can be persuaded?

2. What gave the early Christians power to bear persecution with joy?

3. What is the effect on the persecutors of witnessing the power to bear persecution with joy? What is its effect on third persons?

4. Did Jesus teach Transforming Power?

5. If so, why has it not been more widely practiced by Christians?

## Suggested Reading

K. S. Latourette, *A History of the Expansion of Christianity*, Vol. I, "The First Five Centuries" (Harper & Bros., 1937).

*The Gospel According to St. Matthew* (Rev. Standard Version), Chapter 5.

# 4 | HOW TRANSFORMING POWER HAS BEEN USED IN THE PAST— BY FRIENDS AGAINST INTOLERANCE

BY THE MIDDLE OF THE Seventeenth Century, Christianity had become a series of dogmas to be interpreted exclusively by the clergy, and woe to the man or woman who deviated from the official line! For the populace, Christianity had lost its spiritual power and violence was required to compel conformity to the prevailing dogmas. In reaction against this spiritual sterility, numerous Seekers banded themselves together in England to "wait upon the Lord" for a clearer light. In the humility of silent waiting, they experienced the incredible tenderness of the Spirit and the conviction of its leading toward compassionate regard for the downtrodden and unfortunate of whatever creed or nation. In the darkness of those times, this was a brilliant light out of which the Society of Friends was born. Those who witnessed it felt driven to proclaim it throughout the World without counting the cost, and to take upon themselves all the suffering which such action provoked.

Immediately, the full fury and brutality of the accepted religions were turned upon them. They were called madmen, heretics, rebels, plotters against the Government. They were arrested on any pretext, fined and deprived of their property, thrown into jail, lodged in the foulest cells, publicly horsewhipped, banished, maimed and hanged. Existing laws against dissenters were used against them and numerous new laws were passed to repress them.[1]

Many thousands of Friends were in jail at the height of the persecutions. They were crowded together in pestilential dungeons, where many died. James Parnell, a boy of nineteen, who

16

died in prison from ill-usage in 1655, wrote to Friends, "Be willing that self shall suffer for the Truth and not the Truth for self."[2] George Fox, founder of the Society, spent a large part of his life in jail. Some of the worst persecutions occurred in Massachusetts, where, upon arrival, the first Friends were arrested and imprisoned, their books burned in public, their personal effects confiscated, and they themselves deported. As a result of this treatment, Friends felt moved to return to Massachusetts to confront religious bigotry with a public witness of their beliefs. After the second group had been imprisoned and banished, laws were passed subjecting Friends to arrest, whipping, imprisonment or banishment for entering the Colony. The effect of this kind of treatment on the minds of non-Christian savages is evident from the remark of an Indian Chief, "What a God have the English who deal so with one another over the worship of their God!"[3]

Despite these laws, Friends returned to Massachusetts and engaged in meetings for worship in private homes. They then sought to give their testimony publicly in churches, as a result of which some of them were imprisoned for nine weeks and whipped twice a week during their imprisonment. Others were imprisoned and banished.[4]

In 1657 further penalties were enacted: ear cropping, boring the tongue with a hot iron, and hanging. On hearing the news of the flogging of an elderly Friend, William Brent, two more Friends, Humphrey Norton and John Rous, immediately went to Boston and suffered the same treatment. Rous and two others lost their ears in public. Two were ordered sold into slavery. William Robinson, Marmaduke Stephenson and Mary Dyer felt called of God to testify against a new law of 1658 banishing Friends on pain of death. They were banished but returned, whereupon the two men were hanged. Mary Dyer was reprieved, but returned to Boston in 1660 to bear her testimony against the law. At the foot of the gallows, she was offered a reprieve if she would return to Rhode Island, but she replied, "In obedience to the will of the Lord God I came, and in his will I abide faithful to death." She was thereupon hanged on Boston Common.[5]

These testimonies bore fruit, slowly but surely. When news of the hanging of another Friend, William Leddra, in the same year, reached England, an English Friend, Edward Burrough, obtained an interview with the King, who issued a mandamus to all the royal governors against capital punishment in such cases and deputized another Friend, Samuel Shattuck, who had been banished from Boston on pain of death, to carry the mandamus to the governor.[6] A similar effort by Friends at Flushing, Long Island, at first resulted in a fierce edict against the Friends by Governor Stuyvesant;[7] but when John Bowne was arrested and banished for inviting Friends to meet in the kitchen of his home in Flushing, the Dutch West India Company, which then ruled the province, insisted that religious toleration be maintained. Bowne was able to return home and when later the colony was conquered by the English, liberty of conscience was insisted upon in the articles of agreement.[8]

In England, the Parliament in 1664 passed the Conventicle Act making it an offense for any person to be present at a religious meeting at which five or more persons outside the household were present, held in any other manner than by the liturgy of the Church of England. The Friends refused to limit the size of their meetings or to hold them secretly. As stated by Richard Baxter, who was hostile to Quakerism, "Yea, many turned Quakers because the Quakers kept their meetings openly and went to prison for it cheerfully." Sympathetic juries refused to convict. One of the punishments was to be sold into slavery, but many shipmasters refused to ship freeborn Englishmen into slavery. In one instance, banished Friends used passive resistance and the crew of the ship on which they were to sail refused to cooperate with the authorities. Out of 55 Friends ordered to be deported on this ship, the turnkeys could get only four of them aboard.[9]

At long last, courage and persistence and the suffering which Friends and many others endured began to win religious tolerance. When James II became King, a royal pardon was obtained in 1686 releasing from prison all who had been unwilling to take the Oath of Allegiance, and also a royal warrant releasing 1400 Friends who were lying in prison. The trade of informing was utterly discredited and in 1687 the Declaration of Indulgences established freedom of conscience for all. Then came the Revolution of 1688. To what extent the nonviolent witness of Friends may have contributed to the fact that this great turning point in history was "bloodless" cannot be ascertained; but certain it is that Friends had declared to Charles II in 1660 that they would never "fight and war against any man with outward weapons, neither for the kingdom of Christ nor for the kingdoms of this world" and throughout the struggle for freedom of conscience they remained consistently faithful to their declaration. In 1689, the Toleration Act became law and marked a turning point in the history of religious freedom. The power of the persecuting spirit was shattered beyond recovery.[10] In the words of Elfrida Vipont, "It is not too much to claim that it had been broken by the heroism of men and women who had refused to be bowed by it; who had suffered without attempting to retaliate; who had faced death rather than succumb; and who . . . had found their strength in the still Spirit that kept them."[11]


## Topics for Discussion

1. What elements in the actions of early Friends contributed most to the winning of religious tolerance?

2. Discuss some specific evidences of the effectiveness of Transforming Power as applied by early Friends to change the minds of persecutors. Of third persons.

3. Was the action of Friends in returning to Massachusetts illegally after they had been banned and warned, non-violent?

4. Were early Friends, as a minority religious group, mor-

ally justified in publicly and persistently attacking the religious beliefs of the majority?

5. Is it in the true spirit of Christianity to fight ideas and actions which are contrary to our consciences, as long as we do not use "outward weapons"?

## Suggested Reading

Elfrida Vipont, *The Story of Quakerism* (Bannisdale Press, London, 1955), Chaps. I-XII.

Howard Brinton, *Friends for 300 Years* (Harper & Bros., New York, 1952, $3.00), pp. 151-174.

# 5 | INCOMPLETE USE OF TRANSFORMING POWER BY FRIENDS AGAINST SLAVERY[1]

As IN THE CASE of early Christianity, success dampened the ardor and power of the original testimony of the Society of Friends. With the coming of religious tolerance, Friends began to feel easy at being just another Christian sect, without a burning concern to spread the tenderness of the spirit through the whole of society. Their reaction to slavery in the United States is a good example of this. Historians have taken just pride in the leadership of the Society in awakening the American people to the evils of slavery, but often have ignored how fragmentary was the vision and action on this issue. Seeing the evils both of slavery and of violence, Friends' repugnance to violence dampened the witness of many against slavery, while their revulsion against slavery dulled the witness of others against violence. As a result, the anti-slavery movement started by Friends was taken over by radicals who believed in violence and were unmoved by the spirit of tenderness. This bred unyielding opposition on the part of slaveholders and led to Secession, the War Between the States and Reconstruction, which have poisoned our national life for a hundred years. It has left us a heritage of sectional jealousies and racial prejudices which plague us to this day. Indeed, the racial issues which now confront us are, perhaps, second in importance only to war. It may well be that we shall have to solve the racial issue first, since it might prove most difficult to transform the enemies of American society while our position is morally weakened by the inequities heaped upon our 18 million black citizens.

It was in 1688, while Quakerism was still young and burning with the urgency of its message, that Germantown Monthly Meeting in Pennsylvania made the first organized protest against slavery.[2] It remained for John Woolman, whose conscience was fully aroused against slavery, to open the consciences of many others in the Society through his witness. He refused to write bills of sale and other documents binding blacks to slavery.[3] He changed his manner of dress to avoid wearing clothes containing dyes which were the fruit of slave labor.[4] In full keeping with the principle of good will toward adversaries, he did not denounce slaveholders as brutal, nor try to impose abolition on them by political or military force. Instead, he laid the question of the morality of slavery before "the Light of Christ" within them and left *them* to answer to God.[5] He traveled extensively through New England, New York, Maryland and Virginia, laying his concern before Friends' meetings, as a result of which his views gained momentum and Friends took the position that the slave trade must end. This soon spread to slavery itself and in 1776 the Philadelphia Yearly Meeting directed that those persisting in holding slaves be disowned.

By the close of the 18th Century, slaveholding by Quakers had ceased, as a result of action by Yearly Meetings in Philadelphia, New England, New York, North Carolina, Baltimore and Virginia.[6] In 1819, the Pennsylvania Abolition Society (composed largely of Friends) declared that the practice of holding and selling human beings as property ought to be immediately abandoned, but only by lawful and constitutional means.[7] We may perhaps detect a falling away from the spirit of earlier Friends in the substitution of the words "lawful and constitutional" for a phrase such as "loving and peaceful."

The unconscious moral torpor bred by commercial prosperity and the growing cotton interests of the country, resulted in a period of stagnation during which abolition societies contented themselves with petitions to Congress and the issuance of declarations of principles.[8] But consciences were again aroused by the burning concern of certain individual Friends, notably Benjamin Lundy and Lucretia Mott, who organized anti-slavery societies, traveled, spoke and wrote extensively against slavery.[9] Lundy organized a meeting to renounce the use of slave products.[10] Lucretia Mott's husband, James Mott, sacrificed great wealth by quitting the cotton business due to its close connection with slavery.[11]

Quakers began to take direct action toward the freeing of slaves by participating in the "Underground Railroad," the cooperative enterprise through which runaway slaves were aided in their escape to Canada. This was in violation of the Fugitive Slave Law and involved civil disobedience for the sake of conscience. When Thomas Garrett, a Quaker leader in this work, was convicted and his entire property swept away, he said to the judge, "Judge, thou hast not left me a dollar, but I wish to say to thee and to all in this court-room, that if anyone knows of a fugitive who wants shelter and a friend, send him to Thomas Garrett and he will befriend him."[12]

One cannot read the history of the witness of Friends against slavery without feeling that if the spiritual life of the Society at this time had been sufficiently deep, Friends would have been moved to a more powerful witness toward a non-violent solution. It took a secessionist movement by abolitionist Friends in forming a new Yearly Meeting in 1843, known as Indiana Yearly Meeting of Anti-Slavery Friends,[13] to arouse the entire Society in America to the real meaning of slavery.[14] But this consolidation of opinion was not followed by active public witness for a non-violent solution. While Friends who operated the Underground Railroad were moved by tenderness toward the slaves, they were neglecting possibilities of confronting the slave owners with action calculated to transform them. Angelina Grimké's "Appeal to the Christian Women of the Southern States" remains one of the few witnesses against slavery which spoke to the better instincts of the slave owner.[15] Though, like all abolitionist literature, the "Appeal" was banned and burnt in the South, it was more widely read by southerners than any other contemporary piece of abolitionist literature. Such expressions of love in action toward those whose views most needed to be changed were quite rare. One can only speculate what might have been the effect on public opinion in the South, if large numbers of Friends had combined to compensate slave owners for slaves whom they aided to escape, had presented themselves on the plantations, and offered to do the work of the slaves who had escaped, to take their beatings and lynchings, and to train the slaves, by example, in the use of Transforming Power in their own behalf. Could Friends have popularized the principle of emancipation for just compensation?

It is easy to judge by hindsight. The fact remains that the heritage of bitterness and prejudice from the days of slavery still persists and the spirit of early Quakers can still move us to tenderness and heroism in reconciling racial conflicts through love.

## Topics for Discussion

1. How do you account for the fact that Friends were much slower and less enthusiastic in their reaction against slavery in America than in their reaction against the religious bigotry of the 17th Century?

2. Would it have been possible to abolish slavery without war and, if so, how?

3. In operating the Underground Railroad, were Friends acting violently toward slave owners? Was this action justified?

4. In what ways could Transforming Power have been applied to persuade slave owners to acquiesce in the abolition of slavery without bloodshed?

5. How can this same power be used to remove the discord which still exists between blacks and whites and between the North and South?

## Suggested Reading

Rufus M. Jones, *The Later Periods of Quakerism* (St. Martin's Press, New York, 1921), Vol. II, pp. 559-618.

Josephine M. Benton, *John Woolman "Most Modern of Ancient Friends"* (obtainable from Friends General Conference, 1520 Race St., Philadelphia, Pa. 19102, $.25), pp. 21-24.

Reginald Reynolds, *John Woolman and the 20th Century* (Pendle Hill Pamphlet No. 96, 1958, obtainable from American Friends Service Committee, 160 N. 15th St., Philadelphia, Pa. 19102).

Gerda Learner, *The Grimke Sisters from South Carolina* (Schoken Books, New York, N.Y, 1967).

## 6 | HOW TRANSFORMING POWER WAS USED IN MODERN TIMES— BY GANDHI IN SOUTH AFRICA

THE GREAT SIGNIFICANCE of the use of Transforming Power by M. K. Gandhi (who called it "Satyagraha") lies in his development of mass techniques which proved their effectiveness in modern times. He did this in face of the fact that he was exposed to the full impact of arguments which favored the use of violence in the two world wars. He was, moreover, a Hindu by religion; and while he found himself in accord with the teachings of Jesus, his success proved that the capacity to use Transforming Power is by no means confined to those who profess Christianity. It also proved the great importance of inspired leadership in any attempt to use this power in a mass movement.

East Indians in South Africa had been discriminated against and treated like coolies since they first came to South Africa as indentured laborers in 1860. Gandhi, who had come to South Africa to try a lawsuit, stayed on to defend the rights of his fellow countrymen. He first used all the usual methods, such as addressing conferences, drafting memorials to ministers, writing letters to newspapers and circulating petitions.[1] Instead of improving, matters got worse and Gandhi barely escaped lynching.[2]

In 1906 an additional oppressive law was proposed to require all Indians to register, submit to fingerprinting and carry a certificate at all times. Gandhi called a mass meeting and prepared a resolution against compliance with the law. In proposing it to the meeting, Sheth Haji Habib urged that it be adopted "with God as their witness." Gandhi pointed out that this would

26

make it a religious vow which could not be broken and begged them to consider their action carefully. "A man who deliberately and knowingly takes a pledge and breaks it, forfeits his manhood," he said, and if they persisted in opposition they might be jailed, beaten, deprived of their jobs and property and deported, but if only a handful were true to their pledge, there could be only one result—victory. The vote to disobey the law was unanimous.[3]

The Act was adopted by the Transvaal and the Indians refused to register. Gandhi was the first to be arrested.[4] He was visited in jail by the Minister of Finance and Defense, General Smuts, who offered to repeal the Act if most of the Indians would register voluntarily. Gandhi accepted this compromise, but was hard put to it to justify his action to his constituents. "A Satyagrahi" (exponent of Transforming Power), he said, is "never afraid of trusting the opponent . . . for an implicit trust in human nature is the very essence of his creed." Gandhi was brutally beaten by some of his followers for betraying the Indian community, but while in severe pain from his wounds he fulfilled his agreement with Smuts by being the first to register under the Act. Imagine Gandhi's discomfiture when Smuts thereupon broke his pledge and offered a bill in the legislature which kept the law in effect!

A meeting was called at which the indignation of the Indian community was publicly dramatized by the burning of more than 2,000 registration certificates. Gandhi explained that his Satyagraha had performed its intended function. It had given the opponent another chance to discard his baser impulses and, on his failure to do so, had consolidated public opposition by clearly revealing the baseness of those motives.[5]

The Indians decided not to register and to defy a ban on their immigration into the Transvaal. Individuals carefully selected to enter the Transvaal from Natal were promptly arrested, as was Gandhi himself for the second time.[6]

The final showdown took place when the Indians were moved to civil disobedience by two developments: a refusal to lift a

£3 annual tax on ex-serfs in Natal, and a court decision invalidating Indian marriages. A group of Indian women who were made concubines by this decision, defied the law by crossing the border from Transvaal into Natal, where they proceeded to the coal fields and persuaded the Indian miners to go out on strike. When the women were jailed, the strike spread. The strikers pitched camp, 5,000 strong, outside the house where Gandhi was staying. He organized a march into the Transvaal which would subject them to arrest; but before moving he communicated his intentions to the Government, stating that if the £3 tax were repealed, the strikers would return to work. In four days of the march, Gandhi and the other leaders were arrested several times. The miners were forcibly returned to the mines, but whipping and beating were ineffective in forcing them to return to work. The strike spread until 50,000 were on strike and several thousand were in prison. The military were called out. At a mass meeting, Gandhi emphasized that this was a struggle for human liberty and religion and urged his followers not to "consider their salaries, trades, or even families, or their own bodies. . . . " He announced another march.

At this point, an unrelated strike of the white employees of all the railroads occurred and martial law had to be declared. Gandhi's method of taking advantage of this situation was to call off his march and suspend resistance until the conclusion of the railroad strike. The immediately favorable reaction to this unexpected act of chivalry turned the tide. Smuts offered to negotiate, stating that "you can't put 20,000 Indians into jail." "Forgiveness," Gandhi told his followers, "is the ornament of the brave." A compromise was arrived at and enacted into law. It embodied the basic demands of the Indians.[7]

The effect of this campaign on General Smuts can be gathered from his words written some 25 years after the events:

"It was my fate to be the antagonist of a man for whom even then I had the highest respect . . . He never forgot the human background of a situation, never lost his temper or succumbed to hate, and preserved his gentle humor even

28

in the most trying situations . . . I must frankly admit that his activities were very trying to me . . . His method was deliberately to break the law and organize his followers into a mass movement . . . A wild and disconcerting commotion was created, large numbers of Indians had to be imprisoned for lawless behavior, and Gandhi himself received—what no doubt he desired—a period of rest and quiet in jail. For him everything went according to plan. For me—the defender of law and order—there was the usual trying situation, the odium of carrying out a law which had not strong public support, and finally the discomfiture when the law was repealed."[8]

### Topics for Discussion

1. Do you think that Gandhi's campaign in South Africa could have succeeded if he had not trusted the authorities and taken numerous steps to show his good will towards them?

2. Do you think that Gandhi could have effectively organized a mass movement in South Africa without making use of the pledge and the religious appeal?

3. Did the heroism, suffering and sacrifice required of participants in the South African campaign tend to increase the loyalty of the participants? Do you think these requirements repelled more participants than they attracted?

4. Do you think the heroism, suffering and sacrifice promoted the willingness of the authorities to negotiate? Would firmness without suffering have accomplished the same result?

5. What discipline did Gandhi expect of adherents of nonviolence? To what extent is good will to the adversary and faithfulness to the cause essential in every action?

## Suggested Reading

Louis Fischer, *The Life of Mahatma Gandhi* (Harper & Bros., 1950), pp. 40-119.

Mohandas K. Gandhi, edited by Kumarappa Bharatan, *Non-Violent Resistance* (Schoken Books, New York, N.Y., 1961).

M. K. Gandhi, *The Story of My Experiments with Truth* (Beacon Press, Boston, 1957, $1.95).

M. K. Gandhi, *Satyagraha in South Africa* (Navajivan Publishing House, Ahmedabad, India, 1940).

Gene Sharp, *Gandhi Wields the Weapon of Moral Power: Three Case Histories* (Navajivan Publishing House, Ahmedabad; 1960).

# 7 | HOW TRANSFORMING POWER WAS USED IN MODERN TIMES— BY GANDHI IN INDIA

"IF WE ACT JUSTLY, India will be free sooner. You will see, too, that if we shun every Englishman as an enemy, home rule will be delayed. But if we are just to them, we shall receive their support . . . " wrote Gandhi in 1909 when he was still in the midst of his South African struggle. This was prophetic.[1] In 1915, he moved to India and prepared to use Satyagraha (which has been translated as "adherence to truth") for the liberation of his native land from British rule. He knew that his message could never be "transmitted through the lip" and announced in 1916 "that we have now reached almost the end of our resources in speech making . . . it is necessary that our hearts have got to be touched and that our hands and feet have got to be moved."[2]

He placed his faith in the ability of the 360 million virtually destitute and unlettered peasants of India to learn, in time, to follow Satyagraha.[3] Identifying himself with their burdens and sorrows, he founded an Ashram, a religious center. Here with his closest followers he lived in simplicity and poverty. They practiced absolute non-violence and the overcoming of religious and intercaste prejudice. As an example of the economic self-help which Gandhi felt would be the salvation of the peasants, they also practiced hand spinning and weaving. Although himself a middle caste Hindu, Gandhi had outcaste untouchables living with him in the Ashram. Various wealthy people gave the money to sustain the inmates in poverty.[4]

After the first World War, the restoration of civil liberties which had been drastically curtailed during the War, was expected. Instead, in 1919, the Rowlett Act was passed to continue the restrictions in effect. In protest, Gandhi suggested a general suspension of economic activity (called a hartal) to be observed as a day of fasting, humiliation and prayer.[5] It was to be followed by an application of Satyagraha. Six hundred in Bombay signed the Satyagraha pledge which Gandhi described as "no small thing. It is an attempt to introduce the religious spirit into politics. We may no longer . . . meet . . . evil with evil; but we have to make a continuous and persistent effort to return good for evil . . . nothing is impossible."[6] While the nation-wide hartal was a complete success in Bombay, it provoked violence in Delhi and finally degenerated into general rioting. Gandhi called off the entire campaign as "a Himalayan miscalculation" resulting from his having overlooked the fact that people must be trained in civil disobedience before it can succeed.[7]

This was not the only time that Gandhi called off attempts to demonstrate Satyagraha when violence occurred or was threatened. He did this a number of times and in some instances waited years before resuming the effort. The soundness of his action on this occasion was demonstrated by the terribly violent reaction which the excesses of the hartal evoked from the British. In a deliberate attempt to terrorize the population into submission, Gen. R. E. H. Dyer led a force of 65 soldiers into Jallianwalla Bagh, an enclosure where a meeting had been called in violation of a proclamation he had issued. He ordered the troops to fire without warning on the unarmed crowd. 379 were killed and 1,137 wounded. General Dyer also ordered that any person passing a street where an English schoolteacher had been attacked by a mob must crawl on all fours. At this spot he erected a whipping post for the public flogging of those who ignored his order that Indians must alight from animals or vehicles, must lower umbrellas or parasols and salute to British officers in certain districts.[8]

In 1920, Gandhi announced to the Viceroy in advance his plans for a non-cooperation campaign which required Indians to withdraw their support from the British Government.[9] The Congress Working Committee then urged soldiers to quit the army and instructed leaders to practice individual civil disobedience. By January, 1922, 30,000 Indians had been thrown into prison. Floggings had become a daily occurrence.[10] After another attempt at mass civil disobedience had ended in violence, Gandhi withdrew from politics for several years and devoted himself to the purification of India, which he had come to believe was a prerequisite to home rule.[11] The three facets of this program were Hindu-Moslem unity, removal of untouchability, and the promotion of homespun.[12] In 1924, he carried out a 21-day fast for Hindu-Moslem friendship. A fast, in his view, was an effort to reform those who loved him.[13] With this in mind, he conducted his fast in the home of a Moslem so that Moslems would see that he was brother to a Moslem, and Hindus that he had confided his life to a Moslem.[14]

By 1928, Gandhi felt the time to be ripe for another campaign of civil disobedience. He selected Vallabhbhai Patel to guide the 87,000 peasants of the county of Bardoli in refusal to pay a 22% tax increase imposed by the British. Carts, horses, water buffalo, pots and pans were confiscated for delinquency. The peasants pulled their carts to pieces, scattered the parts and buried some of them. "Those who have stout hearts and hands need never fear loss of belongings," said Gandhi. Contributions flowed in for maintenance of the struggle. A one-day hartal was celebrated throughout India. After five months the Government capitulated, released all prisoners, returned confiscated land and animals and cancelled the tax increase.[15]

In 1930, Gandhi declared himself for complete independence for India and the Congress instructed its members to withdraw from all legislatures and sanctioned civil disobedience, including the non-payment of taxes.[16] Gandhi spent two months seeking the guidance of the "inner voice" on how to proceed with civil disobedience. The inspiration which came to him was one of the most brilliant in his career. He sent to the Viceroy, through the hand of Reginald Reynolds, a British Quaker, a

33

letter seeking a way out before embarking on civil disobedience. "My ambition," he wrote, "is no less than to convert the British people through non-violence, and thus make them see the wrong they have done to India. . . . If the [Indian] people join me as I expect they will, the sufferings they will undergo, unless the British nation sooner retraces its steps, will be enough to melt the stoniest hearts. . . . If you cannot see your way to deal with these evils . . . on the eleventh day of this month I shall proceed with such co-workers of the Ashram as I can take, to disregard . . . the Salt Laws." These laws imposed a tax on salt, which fell most heavily on the peasants. No concessions were made.

Accompanied by 78 members of his Ashram, Gandhi set out on a triumphal 24-day march of 200 miles to the sea. Throngs joined the march at every village until the small band, by the time it reached the sea, had grown to a non-violent army of several thousand. On the beach Gandhi picked up some untaxed salt left by the waves and thus became a criminal. This was a communication which all India understood. It released a general insurrection without arms. Every villager on the seacoast waded into the sea with a pan to make salt. Contraband salt was openly sold in cities. Congress distributed literature explaining simple methods of making salt. Everywhere people were making salt. Mass arrests, not resisted, were followed by violence on the part of the police. Thousands moving into Patna to make salt were ordered to disperse. They were charged by cavalry, but threw themselves flat on the ground. The horses stopped and did not trample them. An armored car machinegunned another crowd, killing 70 and wounding about 100. From 60,000 to 100,000 political offenders were thrown into jail. Yet, with two minor exceptions, there was no violence on the part of the demonstrators in all of India. Because Indians treasured the Satyagraha movement, and lest Gandhi cancel it, they abstained from force. Gandhi himself was arrested; but the movement continued.

Mrs. Sarojini Naidu carried out his announced intention of

raiding the Dharasana Salt Works. His son, Manilal, under Mrs. Naidu's leadership, headed 2500 volunteers as they approached the Salt Works, which were guarded by 400 native police under British officers. Against orders to retreat, they advanced and were attacked by the police with steel-shod lathis (staves). Not one of the marchers even raised an arm to fend off the blows. They went down like tenpins and others took their places. One group advanced and sat down. They were savagely kicked and thrown into a ditch. 320 were injured and two killed the first morning. The raid was repeated for several days.

These events lost Britain her former moral prestige in Asia and made the British people aware that they were cruelly subjugating India.[17] In the words of Louis Fischer, "The British beat the Indians with batons and rifle butts. The Indians neither cringed nor complained nor retreated. That made England powerless and India invincible."[18]

Many British labor ministers and voters came to favor Indian independence;[19] and the Labor Government in 1930 initiated conferences with Indian leaders.[20] Britain proposed a new constitution for India in which the untouchables would have a separate electorate. Because he felt this would perpetuate the division between untouchables and other castes, Gandhi opposed this with all his might and undertook a fast unto death in protest. To him it was a matter "of pure religion."[21] Urgent negotiations between the leader of the untouchables and Hindu leaders immediately ensued and resulted in a compromise as to untouchable representation, which was accepted by the British Government barely in time to save Gandhi from death.[22]

The most significant effect of the fast was the transforming upheaval among the 250 million Hindus. Scores of temples were thrown open to untouchables. Caste Hindus and untouchables fraternized in the streets and temples. Throughout the country resolutions were adopted, promising to stop discrimination against untouchables. Hindu pupils burned benches formerly reserved for untouchables. Wells and streets from

35

which untouchables had been excluded were opened to them. While the fast did not end untouchability and segregation, the belief in it was destroyed, its practice branded one as a bigot, and the trend toward its elimination was begun.[23] The magnitude of this accomplishment may be judged by the fact that untouchability had continued for more than 3,000 years[24] and had embraced one-fifth of the population of India.[25]

As independence finally approached after the Second World War, the Moslems insisted on the partition of India into separate Moslem and Hindu states and the British refused to force a single constitution on the unwilling Moslems. Gandhi always opposed partition and gave all the energy of his last days in an attempt to bring the Moslems and Hindus together. Both in Calcutta and Delhi, where terrific Hindu-Moslem riots had occurred with great loss of life, Gandhi continued fasts which ultimately quelled the riots and brought about agreements of peace between the members of the two religions.[26]

A week after the end of his fast in Delhi, Gandhi met a martyr's death through the bullet of a Hindu enraged by his befriending of the Moslems.[27] While winning Indian independence through Transforming Power, Gandhi had failed to prevent the partition of India. He had, however, brought an end to the current violence between Moslems and Hindus and, like Mary Dyer on Boston Common, he had been "faithful unto death."

*Topics for Discussion*

1. Why did Gandhi's religious convictions tend to unite rather than to divide the Indian people of different religions?

2. Could Gandhi's methods of communicating his message to the illiterate masses of India, be expected to succeed in communicating a similar message to the population of other countries?

3. Do you think other leaders could successfully use Gan-

dhi's methods of restraining their followers from violence? What is the effect of violent resistance?

4. Do you believe that modern dictators could have suppressed Gandhi's independence movement by greater ruthlessness than practiced by British authorities?

5. By what means did Gandhi's campaign change British public opinion?

6. What was the secret of the success of Gandhi's fasts?

### Suggested Reading

Louis Fischer, *The Life of Mahatma Gandhi* (Harper & Bros., 1950), pp. 123-505.

M. K. Gandhi, *Hind Swaraj or Indian Home Rule* (Navajivan Publishing House, Ahmedabad, India).

Mahadev Desai, *The Story of Bardoli, Being a History of the Bardoli Satyagraha of 1928 and Its Sequel* (Navajivan Publishing House, Ahmedabad, India, 1929).

# 8 | TRANSFORMING POWER IN INDIA AFTER GANDHI
by James E. Bristol and Karen Eppler

A GREAT DEAL has happened in India since chapter 7 was written and this book first published in 1960. Although the events herein chronicled are history, and nothing that has taken place in the past three years can alter them, quite understandably the reader may find himself influenced to ask in the light of recent developments in India whether Gandhi has not been completely forgotten and Transforming Power completely discredited in the very land where it had wrought such tremendous changes. The armed invasion of Goa, the effort to turn back the Chinese armies by force of arms, the present military buildup in India, including the cooperative effort of the British, American and Indian Air Forces in the creation of an "air umbrella," and India's development of nuclear weapons—do these negate partially or entirely the Gandhian experience as set forth above?

It is our contention that these recent tragic developments do *not* in any sense vitiate the amazing and revolutionary results of Mahatma Gandhi's reliance upon Satyagraha to win independence for India. Nothing can alter that chapter in human experience. Since, however, there has been widespread disillusionment in the West as India has resorted to the use of military methods, it seems important to put into proper perspective what has taken place in the recent Indian experience.

Certainly in India there exists our greatest repository of experience with non-violent resistance. Because of this fact we in the West have often assumed rather carelessly that India therefore was Gandhian and also a nonviolent nation. Such was never the case, however, in spite of the fact that many Indians were and are deeply dedicated to peace, and that Pandit Nehru has been an outspoken advocate of peace for many years. Independent India has always had an army and even prior to Goa and the Chinese engagements, has used that army, notably in Kashmir and to bring Hyderabad into the Indian Union.

In addition to this careless assumption many Westerners have also assumed that somehow the non-violent resistance demonstrated in the Indian Freedom Movement is per se applicable to the international scene. Yet this is not necessarily so; certainly it is *not,* as some seem to have assumed, *automatically so.* A fuller understanding of a Gandhian movement that has been consistent through the years may help to make this clear.

We must bear in mind as we observe what the Gandhians did in India in the fall of 1962 under the impact of the fighting with China that under Gandhi the non-violent movement in India was a nationalist movement. The Gandhian effort won freedom for the nation, and there is still among the Gandhians today a tremendous sense of identification with the nation of a nature which many of us in the Western peace movement simply can not understand. Those who were later leaders in the government were in this same nationalist freedom movement, with the result that people out of government in the Gandhian movement have been comrades in suffering, comrades in prison with the very people who were later administering government policies. We have no comparable situation in the West.

The position taken by the vast majority of Gandhians is based on the statement made on one occasion by Gandhi that it is better to resist aggression, tyranny, and evil with violence than it is to be a coward and surrender. (To a number of Western minds this appears to set aside the fact that all of Gandhi's life spoke loudly and unmistakably for a third way—courageous and forthright resistance without the use of violence.) Taking these words of Gandhi, and assessing the country as not now being ready to offer non-violent resistance to an enemy, many Gandhians therefore conclude that it is right for the country

39

to resist with military measures, and that short of using overt violence themselves, they will support the national effort.

Perhaps we have not always understood in the West that for many years the Gandhian movement in India has been oriented toward building a non-violent society, a society which will no longer contain within itself the seeds of war and violence. Gandhians have emphasized the need for this constructive work, as over against the war resistance which has characterized the peace movement in the West. In this constructive effort the Gramdan and Bhoodan Movement led by Vinoba Bhave has played a prominent part. Since Vinoba has consistently claimed that Gramdan is essentially the soundest of defense efforts, it now ties in readily with the determination to increase production and to establish greater unity in support of the military program. Accordingly, the Gandhians in the fall of 1962 welcomed with enthusiasm this new opportunity to press on with greater vigor than before in building a non-violent society, nor were they dismayed by the fact that they built this non-violent society in order to give strength and sinew to the prosecution of a violent defense and war effort.

Thus the Indian followers of Gandhi did not challenge the war effort in the sense that many Western pacifists do. True, they will not use guns; they will not kill people; they will oppose military training, even for a segment of society; they were sickened by the arming of civilians, and the commencement in 1962 of rifle drills for men and women, but in these critical days they were equally clear that under the impact of the emergency they wanted to unite with their countrymen in ways short of actual military involvement in order to promote and support the national defense effort.

From the moment the Chinese attacked in October, 1962, however, a small group of Gandhians insisted that some form of non-violent resistance should be offered to the Chinese invasion, that they must provide an alternative to armed resistance. Some felt that a Shanti Sena (Peace Army) should proceed to the border to oppose the Chinese non-violently. There was also a realization that perhaps a Shanti Sena could function effectively only by placing itself in the territory between the two armies, in that way not opposing either army more than the other, but trying to bring an end to the operations of both military bodies. These and related questions were earnestly discussed, but a cease-fire was called before any action could be taken.

In the summer of 1963 Jayaprakash Narayan, a prominent Gandhian leader, proposed that the Shanti Sena prepare itself to act as a peace army dedicated to the cessation of all wars. He visualized this army as a nonpartisan force standing courageous and unarmed between the combatants. Vinoba Bhave shared this dream, but sadly admitted that India is not yet ready. "How can I think of practicing Satyagraha on an international issue," he asked, "when my country has not demonstrated its faith in non-violence? Every other day there is violence by the people, every other day the police resorts to firing. Do you think we have the right to teach non-violence to others?"[1] The possibility of the United Nations organizing an international Shanti Sena was raised in 1971, but today this peace army remains only a hope.

In mid-December, 1962, Ed Lazar, an American pacifist, suggested a Peace March from Delhi to Peking as a tangible way of expressing belief in friendship and non-violence, even at a time of great national crisis and peril. After careful considera- tion the Gandhians asked the World Peace Brigade to sponsor such a walk, and a small international group left Delhi on March 1, 1963, with Peking as their destination. The marchers emphasized friendship for all peoples including the Chinese, and a belief in peace and non-violence as contrasted with war and militarism. Although the marchers were denied entrance into Pakistan and Burma as well as China, they walked through India for more than nine months; their dedication to peace and the proclamation of their message made an impact, strengthen- ing some Indians in their adherence to non-violence, and challenging others to reconsider their commitment to war, military measures, and violence.

As the time grew longer since the cessation of hostilities, and as the war mood abated in India, many Gandhians were able to look more objectively and more critically at the military preparations of their country, with the result that a larger group rejected these outright than was true under the first impact of the Chinese incursion. Much thought was given to the training of members of the Shanti Sena, so that they might both work more effectively in the social and economic development of village life, and be ready to resist non-violently either an enemy attack or enemy forces that might occupy portions of India. Training centers were developed in areas close to the northern border with a view to having men and women trained in non-violent methods of coping with conflict in those parts of India that would be the first to feel the impact of renewed hostilities.

Writing in the October 1963 issue of an Indian Quaker publication, THE FRIENDLY WAY, Marjorie Sykes, for many years both an Indian citizen and a dedicated Gandhian, said: "The Shanti Sainik (Peace Soldier) is thus concerned not only with the defense of a town or village against faction fights and hooligan anti-social elements, but also with militarism in international relationships. The conflict with China has forced the whole movement to face the challenge to nonviolence in 'national defense.' During the crisis many members tended to think of their work as a contribution to the integration and morale of the nation, and so as part of the overall defense effort, complementary to military defense. By February, however, in a discussion of the relationship of Shanti Sena to the Government-sponsored Village Volunteer Force (which concerns itself, like the Gandhian worker, with food-production, education and defense), The Executive Committee declared that 'Shanti Sainiks should preserve the distinctiveness of their stand for the nonviolent resolution of *all* conflict...The power of nonviolence is not meant to secure victory in a conflict for any party, but only to establish truth and friendship. Our relationship with any part of the National Defense Programme must be governed by this principle.'"

42

The first task of the Shanti Sena, therefore, must be the creation of a non-violent India. This requires both daily community work alleviating suffering and oppression, and in times of domestic conflict the job of peacemaker. These two roles are inseparable since it is the dedication of "Peace Soldiers" to the needs of the Indian people that assures them respect within the community. Without that respect there would be little hope of quelling riots or resolving conflicts. The constructive work of the Shanti Sena ranges from feeding the hungry, educating people about the dangers of nuclear weapons and improving sanitation, to rendering relief services to victims of natural calamities.

In 1964 the Shanti Sena was required to test its role as a peace maker. Hindu and Moslem Indians had long lived in mutual distrust. Communal riots broke out in many cities in Eastern India with Hindus angrily destroying Moslem homes. The Shanti Sena was not organized to confront such hatred. Most of the Peace Soldiers lived in rural areas. When the riots began in Calcutta they traveled to the city independently and began working to quell the riots. Despite the lack of united action, individual Peace Soldiers went into the streets to talk with the rioters in the hope of allaying their anger and fears. When the riots were finally over the Peace Soldiers met together and prepared themselves for the difficult task of restoring faith and harmony to the devastated city. Moslems who had lost their homes were given shelter. Peace Soldiers went to live in Moslem neighborhoods, giving those who had fled confidence to return. Blankets and food were provided for the refugees. Lastly, the Shanti Sena undertook the enormous task of cleaning the city. Debris from the riots and the stoppage of all normal sanitation activities had created unhealthy conditions. Sanitation work had always been viewed with contempt in India, and was traditionally left for the lowest caste: the untouchables. The Shanti Sena began cleaning the filth from the gutters. Their example convinced others to join them and soon Moslems and Hindus were working together to rehabilitate the city.

By 1969 the Shanti Sena had grown to 7000 volunteers, including urban Peace Soldiers. Learning from past riots, they had become much better organized. When the most violent riot of the decade broke out in Ahmedabad it took only two days for the Shanti Sena to begin to work cohesively to stop the violence. Shanti Sena took Moslems into their homes, walked from house to house dispelling rumors and listening to the people's anger and questions. They showed themselves to be impartial, caring about the fears of Hindus as well as the suffering of the minority. The example of these respected men and women, and their loving, but insistent demand that the riots stop did much to relieve the tension in the community.

As Ahmedabad returned to normality the Shanti Sena once again offered their services to the community: lending their own money to people whose means of livelihood had been destroyed, distributing food and blankets, doing sanitation work, raising money to rebuild houses, setting up a communal home for Moslem widows...the effectiveness of Shanti Sena activities in Calcutta, Ahmedabad and many other cities is proof that Satyagraha has not died with Gandhi.

Faced with violence, poverty and prejudice, Gandhians are still striving to build a non-violent society. Their belief in the strength of Transforming Power has not waned, and as the Shanti Sena continues to grow, and to work, so does the conviction that someday India shall truly become a non-violent nation. In Gandhi's own words:

The world of tomorrow will be, must be, a society based on non-violence. That is the first law; out of it all other blessings will flow...I see no poverty in the world of tomorrow, no wars, no bloodshed. [2]

Thus the picture in India today is far from clear. Although those in the Gandhian movement are not all of one mind, they have by no means completely forsaken their belief in the transforming power of love and non-violence. The vast majority of Gandhians eschew personal involvement in the use of violence. In a complex and difficult situation they are striving to find their way, undertaking to build even today a non-violent society, with an increasing number giving themselves to the creation of a Shanti Sena which hopefully may deal in the near future with internal domestic strife, and at a future date with larger international conflicts.

## Topics for Discussion

1. Have we in the West been unwilling to come to grips with the Gandhian insistence upon the need for building a non-violent society?

2. Must we renounce privilege and possessions and surrender the concept of nationalism before we can engage in non-violent practice or even move toward a genuine world community based on world law?

3. Is it at all realistic to believe that we can transform the power relations that have brought us to the place where we are?

4. How do we prepare for participation in non-violent action?

## Suggested Reading

Narayan Desai, *Towards a Nonviolent Revolution* (Indian Press Pub. Ltd., Varanasi, India, 1972).

Vinoba Bhave, translated by Bharatan Kumarappa, *Principles of a Non-Violent Political Order* (Kashi, Akhil Barat Sarva-Seva-Sangh-Praksham, India, 1959).

Vinoba Bhave, translated by Vasant Nargolkar, *Revolutionary Sarvodaya: Philosophy for the Remaking of Man* (Bombay, Bharatiya Vida Bharan, India, 1964).

# 9 HOW TRANSFORMING POWER WAS USED IN MODERN TIMES— AGAINST HITLER

THE MERE FACT that Transforming Power was successful against the British does not prove, of course, that it would work against a ruthless dictator like Hitler. We have seen that it was successful against the Roman emperors and the cruel bigots of the Seventeenth Century; but what about the 6,000,000 Jews murdered by Hitler? They did resist, sometimes non-violently, but it was not on a massive scale or usually well organized. Gandhi wrote of this problem in 1938, "If I were a Jew and were born in Germany. . .I would claim Germany as my home even as the tallest gentile German might, and challenge him to shoot me or cast me in the dungeon . . . I . . . would have confidence that in the end the rest were bound to follow my example. . . . If the Jewish mind could be prepared for voluntary sacrifice, even a general massacre could be turned into deliverance. I am convinced that if someone with courage and vision can arise among them to lead them in non-violent action, the winter of their despair can in the twinkling of an eye be turned into the summer of hope. And what has today become a degrading man-hunt can be turned into a calm and determined stand offered by unarmed men and women possessing the strength of suffering given to them by Jehovah."[1]

After the event, in 1946, Gandhi characterized the massacre of the Jews as "the greatest crime of our time. But," he said, "the Jews should have offered themselves to the butcher's knife. They should have thrown themselves into the sea from cliffs. It would have aroused the world and the people of Germany . . .

as it is, they succumbed anyway in their millions."[2] Hitler succeeded in keeping the details of his gas chamber and concentration camp atrocities very quiet at the time so that the full horror of his actions was not known, even to many Germans, until the Allies liberated the prisoners. Open mass sacrifice by the Jews might well have deprived him of the support of his own people. But without experience or faith in the techniques of non-violent resistance, the Jews of Germany were helpless before Hitler.

Let us now see how the spontaneous employment of non-violent action against Nazism by the Norwegians had a very different result. After the Nazi conquest of Norway in April, 1940 and the establishment of Quisling as dictator, some underground newspapers were started. School children and others began wearing paper clips and other emblems as symbols of unity. The youth in the athletic clubs stopped all activity as soon as the Nazis tried to take control of the clubs. When the Germans sought to reshape the laws, all the members of the Supreme Court resigned. Haaken Holmboe, a teacher who had read a little about Gandhi, began to tell others about non-violent resistance, and as it grew, imprisonment, torture and killing by the Nazis only strengthened it.

In an effort to start a corporate state, beginning with the teaching profession, Quisling established a new teachers' organization, headed by the chief of his secret police. The teachers agreed among themselves to resist joining Quisling's party, the introduction of its propaganda into the schools and all collaboration with Quisling's youth movement. On February 20, 1942, between 8,000 and 10,000 of the total of 12,000 teachers, each wrote to the Education Department a statement declaring it to be against his conscience to participate in education as outlined by the Youth Service and refusing to be a member of the new teachers' organization. On February 24 the Bishops of the State Church resigned their posts but continued their religious duties, and 150 university professors protested the Youth Movement.

The Government threatened to discharge the teachers and

closed the schools for a month. It announced that teachers who had not complied by March 15 would lose their jobs, pay and pensions. None complied. About 1,000 men teachers were arrested, including Holmboe. Nearly all the clergy then resigned their jobs. Their leaders were sent to prison and concentration camps. About 650 of the teachers were sent to a concentration camp. From an undisclosed source their families received the equivalent of their salaries throughout their detention. They were put on rations of four small slices of bread a day. Each day they were compelled to crawl and run in deep snow for an hour and a half, followed by another hour and a half of heavy work, and then a third hour and a half of crawling or running in the snow. They thus earned a meal of hot water. After two days of this, 76 of the older teachers were questioned, but not one of them gave in. After several days more, 637 imprisoned teachers were asked to retract. Only 32 did so. The terrorism was resumed. Then they were deported to Kirkenes in the far North, where there were no beds or furniture. They were put to work unloading ships seven days a week. One was killed and three injured.

Realizing that if he became harsher with the teachers, the resistance of the rest of the country would become unmanageable, Quisling gradually released those who were in prison and permitted them to teach without recanting their principles. "You teachers have destroyed everything for me," he said.

One of the leaders, Diderich Lund, wrote afterwards of the Norwegian resistance movement that secrecy was not as effective as bold forthright candor and adherence to open truth. Those who resisted in this spirit were filled with a "strange feeling of quiet happiness . . . even under hard and difficult conditions . . . above all we need efficiency and wisdom, courage and readiness to self-sacrifice. If we possess to some degree these qualities, non-violent resistance will give us the sure and joyful knowledge of fighting in the cause of justice and love. And we shall also know that our fight is the only one leading to lasting victory."[3]

The Norwegian teachers wrought the most successful non-violent campaign of the second World War. They were not, however, alone. All over Europe small disorganized activities non-violently disrupted Nazi plans. Strikes were common. In Holland, farmers and factory workers organized a joint strike in 1943, successfully crippling the Dutch economy, and making it difficult for the German army to acquire needed supplies. Throughout the war Dutch munitions industries were purposefully inefficient. A similar slowdown in Czechoslovakian military output seriously hindered the speed with which supplies could be gotten to German troops in Russia. In Denmark a general strike was used to pressure the Nazis to withdraw martial law. The strike was moderately successful and Nazi concessions, though retaining the right to maintain a military presence in Denmark, allowed the Danish government to remain the official governing body.

Noncompliance was widely used as a means of protecting the Jews. The stories of families which bravely sacrificed their own security in order to hide Jewish friends, neighbors and even strangers are quite common. The town of Chambon, in France, successfully hid its entire Jewish population. The town leaders were repeatedly threatened, and two pastors and the headmaster of the local school were even arrested; nevertheless, they refused to cooperate with the Vichy police. When eventually one Jewish man was apprehended, the entire village brought gifts and sympathy, clearly demonstrating that they considered this man a friend. The police realized that the town was opposed to his arrest, and under the pressure of their friendliness liberated him. They remained in the town another month, but no serious efforts to locate the Jews were made.[4]

Even those who did not have the courage or organization to openly hinder Nazi efforts took part in symbolic acts of resistance. The wearing of hats, flowers, even straight pins, as tokens of anti-Nazi sentiments, was widespread. Many Gentiles chose to wear modified yellow stars as an expression of their solidarity with the Jewish people. In Norway, King Haakon's

70th birthday was widely celebrated, despite the monarch's being in exile. King Christian of Denmark declared a national holiday to mark the 50th year of his reign, and though by this time his government was little more than a Nazi puppet, the day was honored with patriotic jubilation. Festivities such as these served as reminders of national independence, and buoyed the desire for liberation.

Certainly no one can argue that these actions were at all decisive in stopping the spread of Nazism. However, none of these attempts at non-violent resistance grew out of a strategic understanding of non-violence. Those who chose to resist the Nazis did so without an ideological faith in Transforming Power. Viewing these small successes one can but wonder what effect a large, well-organized force of Transforming Power could have had against Hitler's military force.

## Topics for Discussion

1. Do you think that Hitler would have been able to carry through his persecutions against the Jews if they had practiced Transforming Power? If not, why?

2. Why did Quisling feel it necessary to permit the teachers to return to work without recanting?

3. Do you think that open non-violent resistance to a tyrant is more effective than secret underground resistance? If so, why?

4. What might have been the ultimate outcome of the practice of Transforming Power in Norway if Hitler had won the war?

## Suggested Readings

Richard B. Gregg, *The Power of Non-Violence* (Schoken Books, New York, N.Y., 1966).

Gene Sharp, *The Politics of Nonviolent Action* (Porter Sargent pub., Boston, 1973). Consult index for oppositions to Hitler.

# 10 | HOW TRANSFORMING POWER WAS USED IN MODERN TIMES—AGAINST RACE PREJUDICE IN AMERICA

ON DECEMBER 1, 1955 Mrs. Rosa Parks, a black seamstress, was riding home from work on a bus in Montgomery, Alabama. Weary from the day's work, she was sitting in the first seat behind the section reserved for whites. The bus filled up. More white passengers boarded and the bus operator, as required by the segregation laws, ordered her to give her seat to a white man. Quietly, she refused and was thereafter arrested.[1] As news of this incident spread through the black community in Montgomery, the feeling grew that the time had come to protest and it was decided to boycott the buses. The boycott was organized by the civic leaders of the black community in the churches and under the guidance of the ministers. The Montgomery Improvement Association was organized to conduct the struggle and the Rev. Martin Luther King, Jr., was elected president.[2]

At the first mass meeting, King said that while the White Citizens Councils and the Ku Klux Klan were "protesting for the perpetuation of injustice in the community, we are protesting for the birth of justice; . . . in our protest there will be no cross burnings. No white person will be taken from his home by a hooded Negro mob and brutally murdered. There will be no threats and intimidation. . . . Our method will be that of persuasion, not coercion . . . we must hear the words of Jesus echoing across the centuries: 'Love your enemies, bless them that curse you, and pray for them that despitefully use you' . . . as Booker T. Washington said, 'Let no man pull you so low as to make you hate him.'" The meeting unanimously passed a resolution calling on the blacks not to resume riding the

51

buses until (1) courteous treatment by the drivers was guaranteed, (2) passengers were seated on a first-come, first-served basis, blacks seating from the back toward the front and whites vice versa, and (3) black bus operators were employed on predominantly black routes.[3]

The boycott was nearly 100% effective from the start. Handbills were circulated and black taxi companies agreed to transport blacks for the price of the bus fare.[4] Opposition measures were increased as the boycott was prolonged. The police commissioner ordered the black cab companies to charge the legal minimum fare of 45¢. Volunteer car pools took the place of cabs.[5] Contributions poured in from all over the world.[6] Meetings were held twice a week for several months, then reduced to once a week. At these meetings King told the people about Gandhi and his philosophy.[7] "The tension in this city is not between white people and Negro people," he said, "the tension is, at bottom, between justice and injustice. . . . We are out to defeat injustice and not white persons who may be unjust."[8] The people responded with amazing ardor.

The authorities held conferences with the blacks, but refused to yield to their demands. The whites spread false rumors about the black leaders.[9] They announced a settlement which had not occurred in the hopes of tricking the blacks back onto the buses.[10] Then they started a "get-tough" policy, consisting of a series of arrests for minor and imaginary traffic violations. King himself was arrested but released when a large crowd collected in front of the jail.[11] A campaign of threatening telephone calls, letters and postcards was intensified. Finally, King's house was bombed. Fortunately, there were no injuries. An angry crowd gathered. Some of the blacks were armed. "If you have weapons, take them home," King told them. "We must meet violence with non-violence. . . . We must love our white brothers no matter what they do to us."[12]

Two nights later a stick of dynamite was thrown on the lawn of E. D. Nixon.[13] A law against boycotts was discovered, under which more than 100 blacks were indicted, including King.[14] The blacks went voluntarily to the sheriff's office to be arrested. At the trial they testified as to the abuses they had received on the buses. According to the testimony, one man had been shot and killed by a policeman for refusing to leave a bus until he got his fare back. Another, who was blind, had been dragged along the ground when the driver slammed the door on his leg and started the bus; still another had been driven off a bus at the point of a pistol because he did not have the right change. Despite the testimony, King was convicted of participating in an illegal boycott and fined $500.[15]

The blacks filed a suit in the Federal Court asking an end to bus segregation on the grounds that it was contrary to the Fourteenth Amendment of the Federal Constitution. The suit was successful, but the City appealed to the Supreme Court.[16] In the meantime, the liability insurance on the cars in the pool was cancelled, but the blacks got new insurance from Lloyd's of London. The City then filed a petition in the State Court to enjoin the operation of the car pools. During the hearing, the news arrived that the Supreme Court had affirmed the order of the Federal Court declaring bus segregation unconstitutional. Nevertheless, the State Court enjoined the motor pool. At a mass meeting, the blacks decided to call off the protest but to refrain from riding the buses until the Supreme Court's mandate reached Alabama.

That night the Ku Klux Klan rode through the black community—the usual signal for blacks to retire and put out their lights. This time the blacks came out on their porches with the lights on and fearlessly watched the ride. A few waved. After several blocks the Klansmen disappeared.[17] They had lost their power to terrify. One cold night a black boy was even seen warming his hands at a burning cross.[18]

A strenuous effort was made to train the blacks how to behave when integrated bus service was resumed. A mimeographed list of 17 suggestions was circulated. Typical of these was the following: "If cursed, do not curse back. If pushed, do not push back. If struck, do not strike back, but evidence love and good will at all times."[19]

On resumption of service, after a few days of peaceful compliance there was a reign of terror. Buses were fired on. A teen-age black girl was beaten by four or five white men. One black woman was shot. The Ku Klux Klan rode again. The houses of two black ministers and four black churches were bombed. The damage to churches was $70,000. All buses were ordered off the streets. The People's Service Station and Cab Stand and the house of a black hospital worker were bombed.

Finally, the City began to investigate in earnest. Seven white men were arrested and five indicted. Two signed confessions but were nevertheless acquitted;[20] and the others were set free in an amnesty that cancelled the cases against the blacks arrested under the anti-boycott law.[21] This prosecution, however, effectively stopped the disturbance and desegregation on the buses became an accomplished fact.[22]

The situation was summed up by Martin Luther King in the following words:

"The Negro, once a helpless child, has now grown up politically, culturally and economically. Many white men fear retaliation. The job of the Negro is to show them that they have nothing to fear, that the Negro understands and forgives and is ready to forget the past. He must convince the white man that all he seeks is justice *for both himself and the white man*. A mass movement exercising non-violence is an object lesson in power under discipline, a demonstration to the white community that if such a movement attained a degree of strength, it would use its power creatively and not vengefully."[23]

The successful use of non-violence in Montgomery, Alabama, marked the beginning of this mass movement. During the next thirteen years the civil rights movement would grow to encompass a great variety of non-violent strategies, to include blacks and whites, to confront the racial oppression in the North as well

54

as in the South.

On February 1st, 1960, four black students in Greensboro, North Carolina, decided that they had wasted too much time talking about injustice. The time had come to do something about it. Of course they knew about Martin Luther King, but when they decided to demand service at Woolworth's "Whites Only" lunch counter they were not thinking about King or even non-violence. On that first day they were simply trying to dramatize the inequity of segregation. The four entered Woolworth's, and sat down at the lunch counter. The waitress refused to serve them and the students refused to leave. The next day over twenty-five students occupied all the seats at Woolworth's. The sit-in movement grew rapidly. At its height there were over ten thousand people sitting-in at every segregated restaurant and lunch counter in Greensboro. Unwilling to serve blacks and unable to serve whites, management relented and within a year all of Greensboro's theaters and restaurants were desegregated.

By this time non-violence had become a central part of the sit-in ideology. As Franklin McCain, one of the original students, explained,

> We wanted to make it clear to everybody, that it was a movement that was seeking justice more than anything else and not a movement to start a war...We knew that probably the most powerful and potent weapon that people have literally no defense for is love.[24]

From Greensboro, sit-ins spread all over the South, hitting supermarkets, movie theaters, and any place that practiced segregation. As the presidential elections approached, the sit-ins took on national importance. Martin Luther King participated in the sit-in movement in Atlanta. After King asked to be served at a segregated lunch counter, Dekalb County revoked his probation for a driver's license infraction. For this trivial offense King was placed in a maximum security prison for four months of hard labor. Robert Kennedy asked the judge to reconsider and John Kennedy called Coretta King to express his sympathy. Small things, but significant two weeks before the election. Many claim that Kennedy's victory depended on the support he won from the black population.

The Congress of Racial Equality (CORE) attempted to expand the localized sit-ins into a national movement. With this as his goal, James Farmer led the first Freedom Ride: a bus trip from Washington, D.C., to Jackson, Mississippi, in which the passengers, white and black, consciously violated the segregation laws at every station stop on their jurney southward. In theory the Freedom Rides were not much different from the sit-in movement. In practice, however, they were the beginning of a new phase of the civil rights movement.

The violence of the Ku Klux Klan in Montgomery had been sporadic and ineffective in its attempt to intimidate the boycotting blacks. The sit-in movement was met by white stubbornness and anger, but very little violence. Black victories in these campaigns roused white southerners, and as CORE prepared for the ride, southern mobs prepared to meet them. All through May, 1961, Freedom Riders boarded buses in Washington. Every few days the buses were ambushed. A white mob in Anniston, Alabama, set fire to one bus. The riders were brought to the local hospital, but the doctors there refused to treat them. The same day another bus of Freedom Riders was attacked in Birmingham. The police of that city promised the KKK that they would allow the mob to beat the riders for fifteen minutes before intervening. In Montgomery this scene of white violence was repeated. The public was so outraged by these stories of white violence that President Kennedy ordered the National Guard to protect the Freedom Riders for the remainder of their journey.[25]

White reaction to the Freedom Rides marked the beginning of an era of white violence and black courage. Television coverage of white cruelty convinced America that the oppression of black Americans was real. Even more dramatic than the mobs which attacked the Freedom Riders was the violence with which southern police met black non-violent protestors. In Birm-

56

ingham, Alabama, the movement began as merely another protest against segregation. On April 12th 1963, Dr. King led a protest march through downtown Birmingham. His arrest produced what has become the most famous document of the civil rights movement: "Letter from a Birmingham Jail." In this letter, King explained the principles of non-violence, and the conditions which made black non-violent direct action necessary. The police brutality which King experienced inside the jail was only a forewarning of the violence to come. The Southern Christian Leadership Conference (SCLC), led by Dr. King, organized a Children's Crusade in which children would lead the marchers. Police commissioner Eugene "Bull" Connor led his men in attacking the demonstrators. Fire hoses, police dogs, clubbings, were used against men, women and children. Television footage of a huge dog leaping on a little black girl outraged the American public. Birmingham's economic leaders agreed to desegregate the city. The release of this plan marked a major success for the movement and the beginning of retaliatory violence, including the fatal shooting of Medgar Evers and the infamous bombing of the 16th street Baptist Church in which four black children were killed.

The campaign to desegregate had been largely successful. SCLC and the more radical Student Non-violent Coordinating Committee (SNCC) decided that the next step should be to insure black voting rights. A march to dramatize the voting rights drive was organized. The demonstrators were to walk from Selma to Montgomery. The marchers, predominantly black, set out. March 7th, 1965, was to become the symbol of police brutality and oppression: "Bloody Sunday." The blacks crossed the bridge leaving Selma. On the other side stood Alabama State Troopers and Jim Clark's police force. The blacks knelt to pray for themselves, and, in the spirit of Transforming Power, for their oppressors. Major Cloud ordered his troops to advance. With tear gas, clubs and horses the troopers turned the quiet rows of praying people into a scene of panic and terror. President Johnson, outraged at this cruelty, submitted a Voting

Rights Bill to Congress. Two weeks later Martin Luther King led a march of black people and white people from all over America from Selma to Montgomery where the movement began. The National Guard protected the marchers during their four day journey. This final march was no longer part of a struggle, it was a march of triumph. On August 6th, 1965, President Johnson put his signature on the Voting Rights Act and made it law.

The assassination of Dr. Martin Luther King shocked America. He was a man who used Transforming Power to successfully overcome segregation and voting discrimination. Blacks in America are still not equal citizens, however. The "dream" which Dr. King preached at the March on Washington has still to be fulfilled in the hearts of a large segment of the American public.

### Topics for Discussion

1.  Can a group campaign in the use of Transforming Power grow out of an unplanned incident and be successfully controlled? If so, how can it be managed?

2.  Are religiously-oriented leaders essential and what is their responsibility? What is the responsibility of other participants?

3.  What technique was employed in the Montgomery boycott which had not been used in the examples of Transforming Power previously studied? What role can it be made to play in non-violent struggles in America?

4.  What principal idea must the black person get across to white communities before his effort to overcome race prejudice can be successful?

5.  Are there times when acceptance of suffering without retaliation brings success to a non-violent campaign?

## Suggested Reading

Martin Luther King, Jr., *Stride Toward Freedom* (Harper & Bros., 1958).

Martin Luther King, Jr., *Strength to Love* (Harper & Row, 1963).

L. D. Reddick, *Crusader Without Violence* (Harper & Bros., 1959).

Howell Raines, *My Soul is Rested: Movement Days in the Deep South Remembered* (Bantam Books, New York, N.Y., 1977).

Martin Luther King, Jr., *Why We Can't Wait* (Signet Books, of the New American Library, New York, N.Y., 1964).

James Peck, *Freedom Ride* (Grove Press Inc., New York, N.Y., 1962).

# 11 | TRANSFORMING ACTION BY THE GROUP

IN FACE OF THE FORCES of evil in today's world, the individual feels there is little he can do to stem the march of violence. The great sacrifices made by individual tax refusers and conscientious objectors, for example, seem to have relatively little effect on public opinion or on the policies of the Government. Gandhi recognized this and withheld the practice of tax refusal until he had trained the inhabitants of an entire county to use it. When this had been done, the technique was employed with devastating effectiveness.[1] Thus, through group action the individual can multiply his effectiveness many times and it does not take a large group to influence a whole community or nation. If today a substantial percentage of the members of the Society of Friends in this country alone were moved into action in support of the peace testimony which they profess, this could well be effective to switch public opinion from reliance on violence to faith in the power of non-violence.

This is because experience has shown that groups using Transforming Power acquire an effectiveness far out of proportion to the sum of their members. Jesus began with only twelve disciples. Gandhi had a maximum of 230 devoted followers at his Ashram,[2] and it has been estimated that even at the height of his power only a few thousand were committed to the full philosophy of Satyagraha. It is generally recognized that Friends have always wielded an influence far beyond their numerical strength, and this influence can be increased with the growth of their concern and firmness of action.

Dedicated concern on the part of a small group is of course

essential, but this is not enough. The group must also be thoroughly trained in the techniques of non-violent action. This training begins with reading and discussion of the methods which others have employed (Chaps. 3-9) and must be followed by practice by the individual in making spiritual power a way of life (Chap. 2). In this way the principles are mastered, but before any particular project is undertaken, there must also be a thorough understanding of the group conduct called for by the particular situation. Thus, in the Bardoli tax refusal campaign, the leaders discussed all foreseeable contingencies with the villagers in advance and suggested the most effective techniques to be applied, such as taking the carts apart and burying essential portions of them.[3] Detailed written instructions were issued to participants in the Montgomery bus strike.[4] Black students being trained to "sit-in" at segregated lunch counters are required to act out schemes of violence in advance in order to prepare themselves to react lovingly. It may be helpful to quote the following written instructions issued at the Nevada Testing Ground Project. These of course were discussed and thoroughly understood by the participants in advance:

## "A GROUP DISCIPLINE FOR NON-VIOLENT ACTION AGAINST NUCLEAR WEAPONS

agreed upon by a group engaged in civil disobedience at Camp Mercury, Nevada, August 6, 1957.

1. We desire to think and act in a spirit of love and non-violence toward all men, including those engaged in the exploding of nuclear weapons.
2. We will engage in civil disobedience against that portion of the laws of the United States by which nuclear weapons are exploded because we feel in our conscience that the detonation of nuclear weapons is immoral and doing great harm to the human race.
3. We disobey the law in complete openness, after having notified the enforcing authorities and with no intention of secrecy or conspiracy.

61

4. We respect the democratic process and by our act of civil disobedience we challenge the rightness of this law and hope to persuade the American people to stop the exploding of nuclear bombs.

5. In disobeying the law, we are convinced we are doing what is right, but if arrested we will make no effort to harass or to resist the arrest.

6. We will continue walking into the nuclear explosion area until arrested, but will stop when the arresting authority orders us to halt. We will attempt to talk to him. If his purpose is to arrest us, we will not harass him nor resist arrest. If it is not arrest we will continue entry. If the arresting authorities engage in violence against us or forcefully detain us without arrest we desire to think and act toward them in a spirit of love and non-violence.

7. If suffering must come because of conflict between men, we desire to take suffering upon ourselves and not inflict it on others.

8. We act here in our own country, but our protest is directed against the explosion of nuclear weapons by England and Russia as well as the United States.

9. We know that people in England, Russia and many other countries, including our own, have been imprisoned for working against war. We act in fellowship with them and all others throughout the world who work to turn the world from war and the preparation for war.

10. We will choose leaders and accept group discipline in this project."

Each project requires intensive preparation. Where not prevented, frequent meetings should be held. Not only should detailed instructions like those quoted above be issued, but the participants should be fully briefed on the worst that may happen to them and those who are not prepared to proceed should be encouraged to withdraw so that all who remain are fully committed to go through with the project, come what may.

Pacifists have an instinctive objection to anything that smacks of the military, and Friends, in particular, are accustomed to proceed only through unanimous group agreement. Hence, there may be a certain amount of resistance among pacifists and Friends to the idea of taking direction from the leadership. In small projects which lend themselves to participation by all members in the planning stages, much success can be achieved by advance group planning and unanimous agreement on rules; but even here the group must be prepared to follow the direction of its leaders when emergencies arise and sudden decisions have to be made in the field. Furthermore, as projects increase in size and complexity, an increasing amount of discipline and willingness to follow the leadership becomes essential. It was not feasible, for example, for all participants in the Montgomery bus boycott to join in the details of the planning, although major decisions were put up to them at mass meetings. Plans and rules of conduct had to be laid down by a steering committee.

When the point is reached that large segments of the population inexperienced in the use of Transforming Power are to be organized behind a movement, as in India, there must be sufficient confidence in the leadership to enable the participants to follow rather unquestioningly its directions *as to procedures*. General approval of the objectives and the commitment to remain firm and non-violent should be obtained in advance from all participants. This can be done by inviting them to sign a pledge to observe these prerequisites. The methods to be followed are then prayerfully determined by the leadership in steering committees with much seeking of the inner light. From such seeking it may confidently be expected that a sense of the meeting as to the best strategy and techniques will evolve. The task of the leadership then becomes one of coordination of the participants to carry out these techniques rather than of discipline in the military sense.

Recent groups opposed to nuclear power have succeeded in maintaining the use of agreement by consensus and a virtually leaderless group process, for decisions of issues not requiring instantaneous action. The membership of the Clamshell Alliance (the first group to use non-violent direct action against nuclear power plants) was divided into small "affinity groups" which reached decisions by consensus. These groups sent their ideas via an affinity group member to the steering committee where a consensus of all of the groups' views was attempted. In this structure leadership rotates from member to member and everyone has a chance to express his or her opinion. Certainly such a method brings Transforming Power into the process of the group itself; this insistence on agreement by consensus ensures that everyone's view is heard and considered. No one can be abused or ignored. Despite these advantages there are problems with this egalitarian system: it takes a very long time and therefore cannot apply when instantaneous decision is required in the midst of an action. Here, recognized leadership is essential.

## Topics for Discussion

1. What are the advantages of group action, as distinguished from individual action, in the use of Transforming Power?

2. What kind of training is essential to group action? How much can be done during the project? What advance preparation is needed?

3. What are the basic principles which should be included in the discipline for any group action?

4. By what methods can a group be trained to employ Transforming Power and what should be its relation to its leaders?

5. Under what circumstances should the individual subordinate his own judgment and leading to that of the group's leaders?

## Suggested Reading

M. K. Gandhi, *Non-Violence in Peace and War,* Vols. I (1942) and II (1949) (Navajivan Publishing House, Ahmedabad, India).

Virginia Coover, Ellen Deacon, Charles Esser, Christopher Moore, *Resource Manual for a Living Revolution* (1977, obtainable from Movement for a New Society, 4722 Baltimore, Ave., Philadelphia, Pa., 19143).

George Lakey, *Strategy for a Living Revolution* (A World Order Book, Chicago, 1973).

# 12 TRANSFORMING POWER IN THE LABOR MOVEMENT—CESAR CHAVEZ
by Karen Eppler

Black Americans have been oppressed for centuries. Their struggle for civil rights is a dramatic example of the capacity of Transforming Power to illuminate social evils and to persuade citizens and leaders to eradicate those evils. The blacks relied on community ties and long, patient commitments to desegregation.

American farm workers are undeniably among the most oppressed groups in the nation. Unlike the blacks, they are a widely dispersed group. The necessity of finding seasonal work has made any real sense of community impossible to achieve. Racism divides white farm workers from blacks and Chicanos, language barriers make it difficult for Mexican Americans to work with their English speaking neighbors, and poverty forces farm workers to worry about tonight's dinner rather than tomorrow's dreams. The task of organizing this divided, homeless and destitute group into a union of non-violent activists seemed impossible.

Cesar Chavez, born to a Chicano farm worker family, made this challenge his life work. Animosity and hostility were at the heart of most past labor actions. Violence and property damage were commonplace. The huge agribusinesses which employed migrant workers were certainly as cruel as any past employers on the American scene, except possibly slave owners. The life expectancy of farm workers is only two thirds that of the average American. Violation of child labor laws and health requirements are commonplace, with some farms hiring one child for every two adults and others failing to install field toilets or supply plumbing for worker homes. Pesticide poisoning is the most prevalent cause of sickness among farm workers, but the companies did nothing to protect their workers from it. Perhaps most importantly, farm workers were not covered by Federal labor relations laws.

Cesar Chavez worked to change these conditions. He chose as his tools the old weapons of labor, but under his leadership, strikes, pickets and boycotts were not characterized by violence and hatred but by compassion and good will. Chavez's dream was the creation of a union of agricultural laborers, capable of negotiating with the growers and improving the lives of these migrant people. He began his campaign on foot, traveling from farm to farm explaining his goal and convincing others to become members of the United Farm Workers Union (UFW). At first he lived off his small savings, but when the money was gone, he begged as he went. The farm workers shared their food with him and, in sharing their poverty, they came to trust him. Despite the Union's growth, Chavez has continued to live the austere life of his people. He takes as his salary only five dollars a week. In a non-violent campaign, the leader cannot exploit the workers. It is essential, Chavez insists, that the leader be one of the people:

> To come in a new car to organize a community of poor people—that doesn't work. And if you have money, but dress like they do, then it is phony. Professional hunger.[1]

Chavez had issued hundreds of union cards. The time had come to face the growers. The first objective was California vineyards. The wine grape growers refused to recognize the union and refused to hold a union election. The UFW called upon the nation to boycott California wines. The idea of a national boycott was important to Chavez because it would not only affect the wine grape growers but would also educate and mobilize many Americans. The boycott, and especially media coverage of cruel labor practices, convinced many vineyards to recognize the union. However, a few major vineyards continued to ignore UFW demands.

Strengthened by this partial success, the UFW decided to call a strike against the Giumaria Vineyards. It was hoped that successfully confronting these vineyards would convince other growers to accept union representation. Chavez spent many days preparing the workers for the strike. He taught them about Transforming Power, how to respond to threats and even blows without violence or surrender. But they were not prepared for what happened. The growers brought up truckloads of illegal aliens to pick the grapes. These poor Mexicans knew nothing about the strike or the UFW. They knew only that they were hungry and had been offered jobs. (The Giumaria Vineyards paid these immigrant laborers even less than they had been paying their usual workers.) Many of the strikers had no sympathy for these Mexicans. They saw only that these new workers were undermining the strike. They ambushed the strike breakers on their way back from the fields and beat them unmercifully. Chavez was hurt by this violence. He was not only saddened by this evil use of force against people who were only pawns of the oppressor, but he was also afraid that the strikers' behavior would alienate thousands of Americans who were boycotting Gallo wine.

With the view of cleansing himself and the union of violence, Cesar Chavez followed Gandhi's example and began a fast of penance. Fasting, he made a speech to the strikers, explaining that the UFW was not merely a union, it was a cause. "La Causa" promised a better world, a world where poverty and oppression would be replaced by equality and understanding. If the UFW was to help create this world, then it must itself become compassionate and peaceful. He told the strikers that he was fasting to purge the union of violence and that he would continue fasting until the violence was ended. The next day, no one was beaten and many of the strikers joined Chavez in his fast.

Buoyed by the UFW's growing faith in non-violence, Chavez announced a table grape boycott directed at the same growers. By 1975, a Harris Poll indicated, 8% of the United States adult population was boycotting Gallo wines and 12% had stopped buying non-union grapes.[2]

As the UFW was gaining power in its action against the vineyard owners, a new and complex problem arose. Lettuce growers signed a contract with the Teamsters Union without a vote by their employees. A contract with a union that did not represent the workers was as meaningless as no contract at all. The Teamsters Union accepted terms which did not better existing working conditions. Outraged, the UFW called for a strike. Seven thousand out of the ten thousand pickers who worked for the lettuce growers walked off the fields. It was obvious that the UFW was the union preferred by the workers.

Because the pickers were too poor to maintain the strike, a lettuce boycott was added to the already successful grape and wine boycotts. This boycott was difficult to implement, since most lettuce heads were not marked with either the Teamster or the UFW insignia. The UFW convinced their growers to stamp lettuce heads and cartons with the eagle, the UFW emblem. Even so, it was difficult to measure the success of the boycott and supermarkets continued to sell non-union and Teamster lettuce.

Chavez decided on civil disobedience: to violate the law against secondary boycotts (boycotts against companies not party to the labor dispute, such as supermarkets in this instance). He began to organize a nation-wide boycott of all supermarkets that sold non-union or Teamster lettuce, grapes or wine. This boycott further organized the general public. UFW representatives travelled all over the country organizing groups of citizens to picket local supermarkets. The campaign became not merely a farm worker struggle, but a struggle which symbolized for the nation the oppressive nature of large corporate farming. With this secondary boycott, the UFW became a national political organization. Chavez went to speak about racism and the oppression of America's poor at rallies against the Vietnam war and civil rights meetings.

In 1975, California Governor Jerry Brown signed California's Agricultural Labor Relations Act, which guaranteed farm workers the right to petition for union representation and the right to vote for a union by secret ballot. In the elections which followed, the United Farm Workers Union won 113 elections while the Teamsters Union won only 24. The workers had voted for Chavez's dream.

UFW still faces enormous obstacles in its struggle to improve the living conditions of its members. But as they continue to use Transforming Power, to talk and to educate rather than to fight, there is good reason for optimism. The UFW has transformed the angry weapons of labor conflicts into non-violent tools for justice.

## Topics for Discussion

1. What methods can an organizer use to persuade diverse under-privileged workers to unite in the use of Transforming Power to improve their conditions?

2. What makes Transforming Power an effective tool in labor struggles?

3. Can fasting be used effectively in the non-violent campaigns in the United States? How? At whom is it directed?

4. What labor action tool can be effective in winning public support for the workers? How should it be used?

## Suggested Reading

John Steinbeck, *The Grapes of Wrath* (Viking Press, New York, N.Y. 1939).

Marjory Hope and James Young, *The Struggle for Humanity: Agents of Nonviolent Change in a Violent World* (Orbis Books, New York, N.Y., 1977).

Peter Matthiessen, *Sal si Puedes: Cesar Chavez and the New American Revolution* (Random House, New York, N.Y. 1969).

Mark Day, *Forty Acres: Cesar Chavez and the Farm Workers* (Praeger Press, New York, N.Y. 1971).

# 13 | TRANSFORMING POWER THROUGH COOPERATIVE ACTION*

IT IS BASIC to the use of Transforming Power that all other feasible methods be exhausted before resorting to non-cooperation, for it is at the point of non-cooperation that moral force is added to love in the effort to achieve an objective. As already explained[1] this is justifiable only as a means of persuading adversaries who are so dominated by selfishness or prejudice that they are not responsive to reason. There is no way of knowing whether one's adversaries will respond to reason except by testing them; and since non-cooperation at first breeds resentment and hardens opposition, we can test the power of love and reason only by trying persuasion first. We are therefore bound to assume at the outset that every adversary will respond to love and reason. Only when this has failed do we reach the last resort of loving non-cooperation and civil disobedience.

Cooperative methods are manifold, limited only by the imagination and inspiration of the participants. In a relatively free society, like that of the United States, the broadest scope is given to efforts to persuade public opinion. Use of the written and spoken word through newspapers, pamphlets, books, letters, meetings, radio or television is permitted and customarily employed for hundreds of causes. The real adversary is the inertia of mass opinion dulled to moral concern and blunted by the ceaseless impact of propaganda from many sources. Increasing ingenuity is required to arouse the consciences of any large number of people. Appeals to political leaders are fruitless if

---

* Cooperative action is used in this pamphlet to include all methods short of non-cooperation.

the support of their constituents cannot be obtained. At the same time, a small and active group can enlist an incredible amount of support by persistence, when motivated only by moral concern.

Public inertia stems largely from the belief that most propagandists are seeking to promote the selfish ends of certain groups. Removal of this belief moves people to action as nothing else can do. This is the secret of the great respect accorded in political circles to the Friends Committee on National Legislation. As unselfish exponents of moral causes in legislation, this group has wielded an influence in Congress and at the White House quite out of proportion to its numerical and financial backing. It has also served to mold and lead public opinion in support of its projects. This is an example of public cooperative action at its best.

Effective persuasive action requires one to use the means of communication most appropriate to the circumstances. One has to communicate to the adversary first one's respect, good will and love for him as a person and then the truth, importance and desirability of one's cause. The spoken word alone is seldom the best means. We all know the importance of visual aids in lecturing. Charts, diagrams, cartoons, film strips and movies are of great assistance. Any means of dramatizing a message may serve to bring it home as no mere arguments can do. The great power of movies, like "The China Syndrome", "On the Beach", and of DocuDramas such as "The War Game" or "Which Way the Wind?" are examples of this. Thousands have flocked to see these performances who would never have attended a lecture on non-violence.

Other methods of communication include such demonstrations as peace marches and vigils. These are valuable means of communicating new ideas to thousands who never expose themselves to lectures, meetings or pamphlets. They arouse curiosity, which leads many to explore the reasons for the demonstrations. Such methods have long been used with great effect in labor disputes. Many people shrink from public exposure and fear the effect it may have on their reputations and business and social standing. One of the chief values of such demonstrations lies in their challenge to the concern and courage of the participants. As a first step in the practice of the personal sacrifices which are essential to the use of non-cooperation, such demonstrations are invaluable. They help practitioners of persuasive power to learn that talking is not enough, that their concern must lead them to act, and that false modesty or fear of publicity has no place in the hearts of those who are concerned to influence public opinion toward a better world. The spiritual elation and relief which comes with fearless public action speaks eloquently of the sustaining power of the spirit.

The Urbana-Champaign Friends Meeting, of Urbana, Illinois, found a most effective and dramatic means of communicating its concern for international technical assistance as a preventive to war. A group of its members taxed themselves 1% of their gross income for 1958 as a contribution to the United Nations Technical Assistance Fund. Imagine the powerful example which might be given if all the Friends Meetings in the United States taxed themselves 1% of their gross income to establish a center to teach and spread the practice of Transforming Power!

Friends have had long and successful experience with the service of love as a means of removing hostility and building good will. Relief projects in many lands, administered indiscriminately to sufferers on both sides of a dispute regardless of race or religion, have done much to build bridges between hostile groups. Through work camp projects in troubled areas, from Harlem to the Middle East, the American Friends Service Committee is expressing love through service to people in need; and this means of communication needs to be expanded indefinitely.

Insofar as political action is the objective, there is a real question whether it is ever necessary to resort to non-cooperative action in a democracy. Our Government is extremely sensitive to public opinion and responds rapidly to appeals to reason when backed by a substantial segment of the public. The problem is to raise the issues in such a way as to induce public debate. There is no doubt that much could be done toward removal of the threat of war if the United States should adopt a peace-oriented foreign policy. It may confidently be predicted that great progress toward achieving such a policy could be made without any resort to non-cooperation by individuals. The success to date of the efforts of groups like the Friends Committee on National Legislation gives reason to believe that a persuasive action group in every church, or even only in every Friends Meeting, actively pursuing cooperative methods toward the achievement of a peace-oriented foreign policy, could bring this about.

The adoption of such a foreign policy, however, might not in and of itself solve our problems. It would surely go far to prevent the rise of a tyrant like Hitler, or an internal violent uprising by a minority group; but it would not guarantee against such occurrences and certainly would not remove the selfishness and prejudice which have caused the resort to violence in racial and labor disturbances, juvenile gang warfare, and crime. Therefore, it seems clear that we must extend our efforts into the field of non-cooperation if we wish to equip ourselves adequately to deal with the problems of violence and war.

## Topics for Discussion

1. Why must we exhaust all cooperative methods before resorting to non-cooperation?

2. Is a group justified in going to great lengths to convince the public that it has no selfish motive and, if so, what are the best methods of doing this?

3. Can you think of several new and dramatic methods of communicating the peace message to the public?

4. Do you think it possible to achieve a peace-oriented foreign policy for the United States by cooperative methods alone? If so, how?

5. If this can be done, is there still need for training in methods of non-cooperation? If so, why?

## Suggested Reading

*Speak Truth to Power, a Quaker Study of International Conflict* (American Friends Service Committee, Philadelphia, 1955).

George F. Kennan, *Foreign Policy and Christian Conscience* (Reprinted from *Atlantic Monthly*, May 1955).

Chester Bowles, *The New Dimensions of Peace* (Harper & Bros., 1956).

Charles Wright Mills, *The Causes of World War II* (Simon & Schuster, New York, N.Y., 1958).

Robert Cooney and Helen Michalowski, editors, *The Power of the People* (printed and distributed by Peace Press, Inc., 382 Willes Ave., Culver City, Cal. 90230).

# 14 | TRANSFORMING POWER THROUGH NON-COOPERATION— GENERAL PRINCIPLES

*Firmness in the right as God gives us to see the right.—*
A. Lincoln.

WE SHALL NOW CONSIDER the methods available to people who are forcibly held in subjection by selfish or prejudiced groups. It was the friendly and non-violent refusal to cooperate which brought ultimate victory to the East Indians and to the American blacks (see Chapters 6, 7 and 9). These are the methods which might have changed the course of history had they been known and practiced by the Jews in Hitler's Germany, the Hungarians, and the Tibetans. They may yet bloodlessly emancipate Africans from colonialism and apartheid. They are of intense concern to Americans as the only known alternatives to the now obsolete means of defending our freedoms against tyrants and as the most effective methods of dealing with majority persecution of minority groups.

Non-cooperation may be defined as voluntary abstention from cooperation with evil, as by refusing to be drafted or to kill through military action, refusing to pay taxes imposed for such purposes, refusing to obey racial segregation laws, and the like. As with cooperative methods, those of non-cooperation are bounded only by the limits of human ingenuity. Methods effective for Indians against British rule are not necessarily those to be applied against a Norwegian Quisling, a dictator, or the Ku Klux Klan. The mere fact that history does not yield us an answer to the best methods applicable to a new situation should not discourage us. The basic principle to be applied is well established and must be adhered to, namely, love and go. accompanied by absolute refusal to acquiesce in evil.

Are non-cooperative measures appropriate against our own Government as a means, for example, of protesting the preparation for nuclear and chemical or germ warfare? We have noted in Chapter 11 the types of cooperative action which we can use to change public opinion; but suppose these have been tried and the public conscience still remains inert. Are non-cooperative methods to change national policy ever justified in a democracy? Some believe they are and have undertaken civil disobedience in several projects. Others question whether this is morally justified as long as cooperative methods are still available. Is the majority position sacred and unassailable except through the ballot box?

Obviously, the majority is not always right; and where a new truth is concerned, it is seldom right at first. The minority must first try all cooperative methods of convincing the majority that its view is the true one; but at some point civil disobedience against laws contrary to its view of the truth may be the duty of the minority. This will depend on the importance of the issue, and the degree of prejudice of the majority.

Friends, for example, felt it to be a duty imposed on them by God to spread their religious views to the colony of Massachusetts Bay, despite the fact they were always a tiny minority in the midst of a majority which wanted nothing of them or their teaching (See Chapter 4). In fact, before the first Friends came to the colony, there may well have been *nobody* there who wished to hear them. This was an extreme example of an outside group feeling called on by God to invade an unfriendly community and force its inhabitants to listen to their message. We believe that history has proved that this concern, based as it was on freedom of the individual to approach the divine source directly, was one which warranted such extreme action.

Few would contend that the concern of preserving the world as a suitable place for human life would not justify similar action after cooperative means had failed. On the other hand, a democracy cannot work if individuals insist on having their way whenever they disagree with the majority. It is hard to justify a refusal to abide by the rules of the game unless one has a concern so strong that it has ceased to be the mere judgment of the individual, but has become a compulsion of a life beyond ourselves—what early Friends would have called a leading of the inner light. If we feel that way about it, we are justified in taking the position that the laws of man must yield to the higher laws of all life. Until our concern is backed by such a feeling, moreover, we shall not possess the enthusiasm, fortitude and firmness necessary to carry it through the stages of civil disobedience.

Even in the presence of such a concern, we should not resort to civil disobedience until cooperative efforts have been carried to the point where it is clear that they cannot, within the time available, command the support of enough people to accomplish their objective. It is on this aspect of the problem that most disagreement will arise. Who can reliably inform us whether we are developing cooperative methods which are sufficiently creative to change public opinion in time to avoid destruction? Every individual will have to try to answer this question for himself and to participate in civil disobedience at the point at which his conscience tells him that direct action against the majority is the only way to secure the future.

In the next chapter, we shall review some of the hitherto successful methods for resisting evil by non-cooperation. It should be borne in mind, however, that no method can be guaranteed to succeed in advance, and while the methods to be chosen will be those which the participants deem to have the best chance of success, the action itself must be more deeply motivated by the weight of the concern than by the hope of success. Unless the position of the participants is basically sound, the action cannot reach the consciences of others and non-cooperation will not succeed. The power of any method to transform depends basically on the truth of the position which it seeks to uphold.

## Topics for Discussion

1. How does an individual arrive at an assurance that the viewpoint of the majority is not right?

2. Do you believe that non-cooperation against the Government is ever justified in a democracy? Give your reasons.

3. What types of action by the Government of a democracy, if any, can be justly opposed by non-cooperative action?

4. What general principles apply to all non-cooperative methods?

5. Is non-violent non-cooperation a good method of achieving any objective? If not, for what types of objectives is it unsuited and why?

## Suggested Reading

H. D. Thoreau, "On Civil Disobedience," in *Walden and Other Writings* (N. Y.: Modern Library, 1950).

Albert Bigelow, *The Voyage of the Golden Rule* (Doubleday & Co., Inc., 1959), esp. pp. 143-45.

M. K. Gandhi, *Satyagraha* (Navajivan Publishing House, Ahmedabad, India, 1951, obtainable from American Friends Service Committee, 2161 Massachusetts Ave., Cambridge, Mass.).

Mohandas K. Gandhi, *Collected Works* (International Publications Service).

# 15 | TRANSFORMING POWER THROUGH NON-COOPERATION— SPECIFIC METHODS

*Court Action.* One of the most effective non-violent methods of combating evils in free countries is sometimes by a resort to the courts. We have seen how a court decision was one of the determining factors in the Montgomery bus boycott (See chapter10). A more sweeping example is the start toward de-segregation in the public schools which has resulted from the decision of the Supreme Court of the United States. Even if unable to obtain a supportive judgment, protestors can use the judicial system to strengthen their efforts. Danilo Dolci, a non-violent activist from Sicily, stated in a press conference that fourteen prominent Italian politicians were involved with the Mafia. Though Dolci lost the libel suit brought against him for making this statement, he used the trial as a platform from which to speak out against the Mafia. Furthermore his brave ex-ample convinced many others to take the witness stand against Mafia activities. By openly sharing their views, hundreds of Sicilians who had been controlled by the Mafia because they were afraid lost their fear. No longer enslaved by fear, they could work together to create a better and more just society. The court trial had freed them and given them strength. It is devoutly to be hoped that some day the International Court of Justice will be given compulsory jurisdiction over controversies between na-tions, just as our Supreme Court now has jurisdiction over con-troversies between our states.

*Picketing and Work Stoppages.* Two methods, common in labor disputes, could be employed effectively in a persuasive action campaign if carried out in a different spirit from that which customarily governs in labor disputes. These methods are picketing and work stoppages. If picketing is conducted courteously in a spirit of good will and truth, it can be an effective means of communication. A general temporary work stoppage in all industries (called a "hartal" in India) is a most effective way of concentrating public attention on a bad situation. Imagine, for example, the moral pressure which could be brought to bear if all women in companies or industries which discriminate on the basis of sex in hiring or pay levels were to refrain from working for a pre-arranged period. Steps like this have to be carefully prepared psychologically by being announced in advance and clearly directed against a specific evil. It has to be made clear that protest groups are ready to negotiate a settlement on any fair basis.

*Boycotts.* The Montgomery bus strike, described in Chapter 10 is a good example of the type of situation in which a boycott can be successful. Refusal of individuals to patronize businesses which practice discrimination would be another example. The United Farm Workers' boycott against Teamster and non-union lettuce, grapes and wine has been an effective tool in the fight for decent working conditions for farm laborers. A well organized boycott can make immoral business practices unprofitable and thus persuade businesses to operate more justly.

*Sit-Ins.* An example from chapter 10 is the protest against segregated facilities in which blacks sat politely at segregated counters, asked politely to be served and refused to leave until they were served. Similar sit-ins have been held at offices of the Internal Revenue Service as a protest against taxation for the arms race, at proposed nuclear power plant sites as a means of stopping construction, and at finished plants to hinder their operation.

*Reverse Strikes.* Picketing, strikes, boycotts and sit-ins when done with love for the opponent, can be effective methods of protesting injustice through economic pressures. Reverse strikes do not employ monetary pressures; rather, they appeal to the sense of fairness in the opponent. In 1956 Danilo Dolci organized the unemployed of Sicily in a reverse strike which dramatized the government's failure to cope with the devastating unemployment of the region. Dolci and his supporters started voluntarily to repair a badly paved public road. The government met this generous aid with police brutality and imprisonment. Nevertheless, this surprising tactic brought the plight of Sicily's poor to the attention of the world. It unified the poor till they were willing for the first time to confront the authorities, and weakened the Mafia, reducing their tortures, causing several Mafia leaders to be ousted from public office and resulted in the defeat of an Italian senator.[1]

*Pledges.* The spiritual power generated by the dedicated members of a steering committee or leadership group can be transmitted in part to the members of the public who will participate in a contemplated action by means of a group pledge, or solemn vow that certain action will be taken or abstained from. The reader will remember the great force that was generated when the resolution to disobey the Indian registration law in South Africa was adopted by a mass meeting "with God as their witness" (See pp. 26-27). Once the pledge is taken, all who have taken it know what is expected of them and that they must act together to carry it out.

*Civil Disobedience.* Civil disobedience means open, considerate, non-violent defiance of some law which is against the conscience of those who disobey it, and is resorted to after all means of altering it have been exhausted. Since the purpose of civil disobedience is to compel others to re-examine the conscientious basis of the law, the proposed disobedience and the reasons for it are widely announced in advance. The law enforcement authorities are given every opportunity to prevent the proposed action and to punish the participants. The necessary role of the authorities in enforcing the law is recognized and they are treated courteously, but opposition to the law is unyielding and its opponents willingly accept prison sentences and sacrifice all rather than comply. This builds a moral force which no law can withstand if the cause is just and the disobedience is sufficiently widespread and prolonged.

*Refusal of Supplies, Services or Taxes.* Supplies and service of all kinds, as well as tax payments, can be withheld from an unjust or invading power, but this also, in a considerate manner, after public explanation of the reasons for the refusal, and with preparedness to suffer in the process if necessary.

*Migration.* Minority groups have also employed voluntary migration beyond the boundaries of the state or country where the evil rule or laws are applied. This method, however, should not be used merely to escape from the laws, but only when the migration will have a tendency to lead to their repeal.

*Raids.* When Gandhi was protesting the salt laws, his followers conducted a non-violent raid on works where government salt was stored. The suffering which the raiders underwent without cringing or complaint, gave India the upper hand in its struggle for independence (See pp. 34-35). Raids and marches of this nature are appropriate in extreme situations.

*Fasts.* Gandhi's most potent weapon proved to be the fast unto death; but this he used to keep strikers steadfast to their pledge, and against untouchability and Hindu-Moslem hostility —not primarily against the British. He himself said that one cannot fast against a tyrant. He looked on the fast as a means of helping those who loved him—those who would rather mend their ways than be the cause of his death.[2] Its effective use presumes that those who fast are loved, or at least respected by those whose ways they seek to change. Cesar Chavez, devoutly believing in non-violence, fasted against the violent behavior of United Farm Worker picketers. Like Gandhi, Chavez depended upon their love for him to convince them to change their ways.

Non-cooperative actions by Gandhi and his followers were often preceded by a 24-hour purification fast, accompanied by meditation and introspection. Prayer was offered for purifying and surrendering oneself to God and for the invocation of spiritual power. While many people in western countries might not be sympathetic to devotional preliminaries of this nature, the leadership group might be expected to engage in something equivalent. Indeed, much prayer and introspection preceded civil disobedience at Montgomery, Alabama, at the Nevada testing grounds, at the disarmament rally at the United Nations, at the launching of the first Trident Submarine, and at the Omaha missile base. Some such activity seems essential to the maintenance of love and courage in the face of provocation, as well as to the development of an inspired strategy and spiritual power.

A much more exhaustive description of specific methods of non-cooperation will be found in Gene Sharp's *The Politics of Nonviolent Action,* Part Two, "The Methods of Nonviolent Action."

## Topics for Discussion

1. Suggest types of situations for which each of the principle non-cooperative methods would be especially appropriate.
2. What is civil disobedience and how should it be used?
3. Under what circumstances is fasting effective? Do you think it would ever be effective in the United States?
4. What is the significance of the pledge and how should it be used?

## Suggested Reading

Richard B. Gregg, *The Power of Non-Violence* (Schoken Books, New York, N.Y., 1966), Chaps. 5-7.

Gene Sharp, *The Politics of Nonviolent Action,* Part Two, (Porter Sargent pub., Boston, Ma., 1973).

Martin Oppenheimer and George Lakey, *A Manuel for Direct Action* (Quadrangle Books, Chicago, 1965).

Marjorie Hope and James Young, *The Struggle for Humanity: Agents of Nonviolent Change in a Violent World* (Orbis Books, New York, N.Y. 1977).

# 16 | APPLICATION OF TRANSFORMING POWER IN THE MODERN WORLD

"WHY STUDY Transforming Power?" Americans may ask. "As a democracy, we are not ruled by tyrants and there is no way we can use it to protect ourselves against violent revolution or invasion by foreign dictators. Is there any immediate need for it in America today?" We have only to read the newspapers or watch television to know that our modern world is one of violence and coercion based on the threat of violence. This is so of many individual and family relationships, of crime and delinquency, racial and religious conflicts, labor disputes, colonialism, dictatorships, revolution and war. Persuasive action as an alternative to violence, therefore, would seem to be the most relevant issue of the day. By making it a way of life, individuals can start at once to remove violence from their personal lives and bring more harmony into family relationships. Groups in work projects can use it to bring love and understanding into underprivileged areas and to counteract discrimination, delinquency and crime.

Is there, however, any way by which Transforming Power can be employed to assure national safety against the threat of dictatorship imposed by a foreign power or by violent revolution from within? It seems tolerably clear that if massive goodwill in international relationships comes to dominate the foreign policy of our Government, it will go a long way to remove the threat of aggression.

What would be the elements of a foreign policy based on massive goodwill? One of its elements is already being adopted on a limited scale. This is the promotion of international understanding through intimate exchanges in all fields of human life—civil, spiritual, educational, economic and, ultimately, political. This offers an opportunity for those of different ideologies to get to know one another well, to discuss and debate the validity of their different ways on a friendly basis. It involves the substitution of massive fraternization for massive retaliation. A second element would be acts of great love and friendship toward adversary nations—tremendous aid in the event of national disaster, economic and technical assistance on important projects. A third element would be joint activity with potential enemy nations to grant technical aid to underdeveloped areas and to conduct research in world projects, such as the exploration of Antarctica, the ocean beds and of outer space. Another element would be an imaginative and not overly fearful drive to get agreement on completely controlled disarmament. A final element would be great firmness and courage in standing by the important principles in which we believe, such as the right of self-determination of peoples, and possibly sacrifices by citizens or members of an international police force in non-violently remaining until death in control of areas like Lebanon or areas occupied by Palestinian refugees. The very real possibility of bringing about such a foreign policy through the action of some groups dedicated to the use of cooperative methods was discussed in Chapter 11.

Many believe that such a policy requires emphasis on deterrence through military superiority. As explained in Chapter 2, Transforming Power depends for its success on the removal of fear and hostility by expressions of good will. Threats of force and violence are quite incompatible with this aim and, therefore, boasts of military prowess can serve only to set back the cause of peace. Our will to peace should be made crystal clear to our adversaries not only through national acts of good will but also through indefatigable efforts to join with them and other nations in a program for universal, controlled, complete disarmament. There is room to exercise firmness in our insistence on fair and workable controls without insisting on a degree of perfection which will prevent agreement. The application of the principles of non-violence (good will, firmness and inexhaustible patience) in the negotiations, offers the best promise of success.

If consistently maintained, a policy of massive international good will would certainly remove the fear by other nations that the United States may use force to change their institutions. This fear is surely one of the reasons for the arms race. The practice by our people of Transforming Power on a large scale throughout the nation could in time make it clear to would-be tyrants that any effort to impose a foreign rule or unwanted ideology upon us would be futile. A firmly resistant people solidly committed to non-violence cannot be governed. The practice of massive good will toward other nations would tend to keep international disagreements from creating ill-will between peoples and to muster world public opinion, even within the dictatorships, in favor of international good will. In time, it could make it difficult for foreign rulers to arouse sufficient hostility to support a war against us.

If these results should not follow, however, or if it proved impossible to obtain public support for such a policy, we might be faced with an attempted invasion or internal revolution. Could such aggression be successfully resisted without violence? We do not know of any instance in which a large invading army was stopped by persuasive action. When asked what he would do in such a situation, Gandhi recommended refusing supplies to the invading army, presenting a living wall of men, women and children and inviting the invaders to walk over their corpses. If they were brutal enough to do this, he concluded, they would not be able to repeat the experiment.[1] There are so many ways in which an army could remove or bypass a "living wall" of unarmed people without slaughtering them that the efficacy of such a procedure may be doubted. Refusal of supplies, of course, could be very hampering and confrontation with loving acts could be even more effective. For example, when the British troops were attacking the Maori natives in New Zealand, one of the tribal chiefs instructed the men to gather unarmed for a council meeting, and the women and children, gayly dressed, to take flowers and welcome the soldiers with songs and dances. The soldiers were baffled and amazed. They followed the women's procession into the village, where the chief, surrounded by the men, met the soldiers with great dignity and friendliness and invited them to feast and counsel with them. After the feast, the soldiers withdrew, leaving the tribe in possession of its land. It is said that this was the last expedition against the Maori.[2]

A similar instance occurred in Berlin in 1920. General Kapp, who had retreated to the Baltic after the German Revolution, occupied all key positions in Berlin with a force of 5,000 fully-armed troops. The Independent Socialists called a general strike and instructed their adherents to fraternize with the soldiers, explain the situation to them and treat them with utmost friendliness. By noon, the streets were crowded and the people were hanging onto the soldiers like flies. The cavalry was sent to drive them off, but without success. No sooner were the Socialists driven off one set of men, than they fixed themselves onto another set. All services were brought to a complete standstill— no traffic, no lights, no power. The invaders were helpless and in three days agreed to withdraw without firing a single shot.[3]

If such efforts to stop an invading army were unsuccessful, our study of the Norwegian resistance to Hitler (Chapter 9) indicates that determined nonviolent action practiced by the people of the occupied nation would in time thwart the occupation and prevent the conquerors from imposing their rule.[4] Faced with the alternative of annihilation in modern war, we are under the most compelling necessity to study, plan and prepare to apply, procedures through which invaders could be overcome by nonviolent action.

Another of our great fears is that of internal subversion—the attempt by a minority to take control of our Government by violence. Surely the first protection against such a threat is so to conduct our public affairs that minorities have no need or cause to coerce the majority. Prejudice and discrimination, economic injustices, slum areas and materialism need to be purged away; and perhaps this effort should be the first concern of those who would practice Transforming Power in the United States. If subversion should occur, however, it can be thwarted by general non-cooperation by the same methods described above as applicable to invaders. We do not mean to imply by this that there will not, for some time, be a continuing need for both internal and international police and courts to enforce protective laws against as yet unregenerated, criminal, insane or violent individuals.

## Topics for Discussion

1. What need is there for the study and practice of Transforming Power in modern America?

2. Do you think a foreign policy based on massive goodwill would protect us from those now considered to be our enemies? If so, why?

3. How could persuasive action be used against a foreign invader? Against internal subversion?

4. Are the principles of Transforming Power incompatible with the maintenance of an armed internal or international police force?

## Suggested Reading

T. K. Mahadevan, Adam Roberts and Gene Sharp, *Civilian Defense: an Introduction* (Gandhi Peace Foundatin Press, New Delhi, India, 1967). *In Place of War: an Inquiry into Non-Violent National Defense,* prepared by a working party of the Peace Education Division, American Friends Service Committee (Grossman Pub., New York, N.Y., 1967).

Mulford Q. Sibley, editor, *The Quiet Battle: Writings on the Theory and Practice of Non-Violent Resistance* (Doubleday Garden City, N. Y. 1963), esp. Chap. 22.

J. V. Bondurant, *Conquest of Violence.* (Princeton University Press, 1958).

# 17 | PREPARING FOR THE PRACTICE OF TRANSFORMING POWER

IT TOOK Gandhi 34 years to prepare India for independence through Satyagraha. How infinitely more constructive and successful were the results than if the advocates of violent revolution had prevailed! Similarly, today much preparation is necessary before a substantial segment of the people will be prepared to practice Transforming Power. As in India, so in America, the first efforts must be toward purification of the national life. We must be purged of the selfishness and materialism, the prejudice, discrimination, injustices and violence which are destroying our spiritual heritage. This can be accomplished by directing Transforming Power against specific eruptions of these evils. Our objective should be, through such purification, to prove that our spiritual heritage can be preserved without reliance on violence against our fellow men. Such reliance in itself tends to destroy the reverence for human rights which is at the base of our heritage.

National purification begins with the individual. Each has an obligation to purge himself of violence by applying the principles of Transforming Power to every problem of his life (See Chapter 2). He has the further obligation to combine with groups in the effort to overcome specific evils by persuasive action and to multiply its power (See Chapter 11). Activities can be fostered by the nurturing of groups in churches, synagogues, mosques and non-religious organizations to study and practice these principles. In time, such groups may develop into volunteer teams prepared to practice nonviolent action against evils in local situations.

The first step in making Transforming Power a way of life is personal commitment. Perhaps our readers will feel led of the Spirit to make this commitment now. Truths never become ways of life until put into practice and this begins with a deep inner resolution to begin the practice at once and to do one's best to continue it without interruption. Joint action by members of a group intensifies the force of a commitment, since each helps to hold the others to their resolution. Members of classes or groups studying Transforming Power may wish now to pause and jointly to take a solemn pledge to renounce all use of violence in their personal and group affairs, to stand firm on all issues of conscience and to do their best to practice these principles constantly.

How can the personal practice of Transforming Power grow into a national movement? In the same way that the anti-slavery movement grew (See Chapter 5). The concern of individuals expresses itself in small groups; many such groups spring up in all walks of life and express their collective concerns, and these groups in turn combine into larger groups, until finally a national leadership center evolves. Each study group that uses this pamphlet is an important link in the process. There are already a number of organizations—The American Friends Service Committee or Movement for A New Society, the Fellowship of Reconciliation, the War Resisters League, and the Women's International League for Peace and Freedom—

The key to good leadership lies in the dedication of the leaders to the principles of Transforming Power. They should not only have thoroughly studied these principles, but should have been trying to live them. They should have faith in the invincible power and intelligence of the life in all men to guide them to participate in such a movement through inspired leadership. If thus imbued, the leaders will be able under any provocation, to stick to the basic principles of persuasion by love, returning good for evil, and remaining sensitive to the guidance of the inner light. This type of leadership, constantly maintained, is capable of winning the confidence and support of the public and the respect and ultimate persuasion of the adversaries.

What types of action might the volunteer teams undertake? Certainly all forms of cooperative action (See Chapter 13) should come first, such as political support for disarmament, protests against preparation for nuclear and chemical warfare, and the promotion of the establishment of world law against armaments and aggression. To encourage personal involvement and the overcoming of fear of criticism, further lawful action by participating in popular appeals, peace marches, vigils, mass meetings and petition campaigns is necessary. Such groups should courageously find means to support minorities under attack. They could join the campaign against crime and its causes, by opposing capital punishment and by participating in slum area work projects. By engaging in other work projects, they could spread love and good will to underprivileged people in all lands.

Under guidance from the central leadership there should also be participation in civil disobedience, in carefully guided and organized projects. At this point, each individual will have to clear with his own conscience whether he should personally participate. Some will feel a clear spiritual compulsion to do so, like that which motivated many of the early Friends. When this call comes, one dare not count the cost nor weigh one's other commitments. Without fear, one can safely yield full and trusting obedience to the inner light. Others who do not feel this leading will have to consider whether they are morally free to participate.

*Priorities.* Many have moral commitments which could be violated by loss of earning power or reputation. Many have spouses, small children, children in college, incapacitated dependents, creative talents in other fields, or obligations to other causes of vital importance which should not be sacrificed except in extreme situations. Much inner searching is required to determine the priorities based on conflicting values. When immediately confronted with tyranny which would destroy the family or other important projects to which such people are committed, most of them would be prepared to make the sacrifices involved in civil disobedience. While tyranny is only a threat, however, the activities of some will necessarily be limited to the study of non-violence, its practice in their personal lives and in group cooperative methods, as well as the support of those who are able to go further.

On the other hand, many will find themselves free to engage in civil disobedience projects and others will be at a stage in life when they can choose their vocational and family commitments in such a way as to permit them to participate. Others will find it possible to make participation a family affair due to a deep concern on the part of all members of the family.

*Motives.* In addition to priorities, the individual will also need to search his motives before embarking on civil disobedience. Does such action appeal to him primarily because of the opportunity to be a hero or a martyr, to be a leader, to be approved by others whom he admires, or to see his name or picture in the paper? Such motives are incompatible with sincerity, which in turn is an indispensable ingredient of Transforming Power. Insincerity is easily sensed by the adversary and destroys the persuasiveness of the action. The only legitimate motive is to maintain the truth as we see it. If sacrifice is involved, that is merely a by-product. In short, we must beware of the martyr complex.

*Suffering.* Those who decide to participate must realize in advance that all methods of non-cooperation may lead to suffering. No one who is not prepared to suffer the consequences should embark on non-cooperation, for without firmness to the end, success cannot be achieved. To many Americans, the idea of accepting suffering—especially from an aggressor—will appear nonsensical at first. We are living in an expanding economy, with political freedom, plenty of jobs and luxuries, drugs to relieve pain and cure disease. We have been struggling to get away from suffering. Why should anyone voluntarily assume it? Perhaps the answer was best expressed by a black woman who was asked by a reporter if it was not very hard to remain non-violent at a lunch counter sit-in while a white mob was cursing and ridiculing her and throwing lighted cigarettes in her hair. She said, "Well, you see, I care so very much about this that it doesn't really matter *what* happens to me." If we seriously face the evils of our day and the very real threat to human survival, how can we avoid "caring" enough to maintain our stand? We cannot maintain it unless we are willing to accept the suffering it may force upon us; and it will give us courage to realize that the very suffering itself is often the determining factor in victory. Suffering may be the price to be paid for non-violence. Willingness to undergo it rather than to yield to an evil or to inflict violence on others is a measure of how much we care.

An increasing number of Americans care enough about preparation for nuclear and chemical warfare to bear the suffering involved in civil disobedience. Others who have conflicting priorities or who do not believe that cooperative methods have been exhausted, or that current dangers warrant civil disobedience, would undoubtedly care enough to accept suffering if the country were actually attacked or occupied by a tyrant. Such people may not be ready to engage in non-cooperative methods today. Nevertheless they would much more profitably study and train themselves in these methods than accept military service—to the end that if tyranny should threaten, America would be prepared to resist effectively and non-violently, as the Norwegian teachers did against Hitler, rather than suffer the fate of the Hungarians or the Jews in Germany.

New ideas, methods and techniques will come out of such study and training and create a public realization that Transforming Power can be more effective than violence to preserve our highest values. It is even possible that in time action teams might so prove their usefulness as to become a qualified source of volunteers for non-violent police groups, for use by the authorities, or even by the United Nations, in troubled situations. This will be a sign of the beginning of the World Community, out of which alone can be realized the aspiration for a "just and lasting peace."

## Topics for Discussion

1. What must happen to our national life before a large proportion of the people will be prepared to practice Transforming Power?

2. How can the personal practice of Transforming Power grow into a national movement?

3. Have you searched inwardly to determine whether you are now prepared to participate in civil disobedience? If so, what are your moral priorities and dominant motives?

4. Why must participants in non-cooperative methods be prepared to suffer?

5. If suffering may be involved, why should anybody participate?

## Suggested Reading

Gerald and Patricia Mische, *Towards a Human World Order* (Paulist Press, New York, N.Y., 1977).

*In Place of War: an Inquiry into Nonviolent National Defense* Prepared by a working party of the American Friends Service Committee (Grossman Pub., New York, N.Y., 1967).

# FOOTNOTES BY CHAPTERS

## CHAPTER 1

[1] R. R. Diwaker, *Satyagraha: the Power of Truth* (Henry Regnery & Co., 1948) p. 1.

[2] This period is given as 30 years in the original of this quotation, but the 70-year period is given in another account, A. Ruth Fry, *Victories Without Violence* (published by the author, 48 Clarendon Road, London, 4th ed.), pp. 14-15.

[3] Allan A. Hunter, *Courage in Both Hands* (Fellowship of Reconciliation), p. 66.

[4] Center for Defense Information, 122 Maryland Ave., N.E., Washington, D.C., 20002.

## CHAPTER 2

[1] Albert Bigelow, *The Voyage of the Golden Rule* (Doubleday & Co., 1959), pp. 219-21.

[2] See Chapters 3-7.

[3] See pp. 35-36.

[4] N. K. Bose, *Selections from Gandhi* (Navajivan Publishing House, 1948), pp. 155-56, 162-64.

[5] Martin Luther King, Jr., *Stride Toward Freedom* (Harper & Bros., 1958), pp. 85-89.

[6] Albert Bigelow, *op. cit.* f.n. 1, pp. 24-25.

[7] *Ibid.*, pp. 58, 114-15.

## CHAPTER 3

[1] K. S. Latourette, *A History of the Expansion of Christianity*, Vol. I, "The First Five Centuries" (Harper & Bros., 1937), p. 369.

[2] *Ibid.*, p. 112.

[3] *Ibid.*, p. 268.

[4] *Ibid.*, p. 274.

[5] *Ibid.*, pp. 137-38.

[6] *Ibid.*, p. 152.

[7] *Ibid.*, p. 162.

[8] *Ibid.*, p. 156.

[9] *Ibid.*, p. 158.

[10] Matt. 5:21-22.

[11] Matt. 26:52.

[12] Matt. 5:38-41.

[13] Matt. 5:43-44.

[14] Romans 12:20-21.

## CHAPTER 4

[1] Elfrida Vipont, *The Story of Quakerism* (Bannisdale Press, 1955). Chapters I-XII.

[2] *Ibid.*, pp. 47-48.

[3] *Ibid.*, pp. 51-52.

[4] *Ibid.*, p. 65.

[5] *Ibid.*, pp. 73-74.

[6] *Ibid.*, pp. 81-82.

[7] *Ibid.*, p. 66.

[8] *Ibid.*, p. 83.

[9] *Ibid.*, pp. 95-96.

[10] *Ibid.*, pp. 124-26.

[11] *Ibid.*, p. 126.

## CHAPTER 5

[1] This chapter is based on a Term Paper prepared by the author's daughter, Margery S. Apsey, entitled "Slavery and the Quakers in America."

[2] Vipont *op. cit.* Ch. 4, f.n. 1, pp. 120-121.

[3] Janet Whitney, *John Woolman, American Quaker* (Little Brown & Co., Boston, 1942) pp. 82-84.

[4] *Ibid.,* pp. 276-80.

[5] Elbert Russel, *The History of Quakerism* (Macmillan & Co., New York, 1943), p. 249.

[6] *Ibid.,* pp. 247-48.

[7] Rufus M. Jones, *The Later Periods of Quakerism* (Macmillan & Co., London, 1921), Vol. II, p. 560.

[8] *Ibid.,* p. 560.

[9] *Ibid.,* pp. 561-74.

[10] *Ibid.,* p. 564.

[11] *Ibid.,* p. 570.

[12] *Ibid.,* p. 577.

[13] *Ibid.,* p. 590.

[14] Elbert Russel, *op. cit.* f.n. 5, p. 369.

[15] Gerda Learner, *The Grimke Sisters from South Carolina* (Schoken Books, N.Y., 1967), p. 146

## CHAPTER 6

[1] Louis Fischer, *The Life of Mahatma Gandhi* (Harper & Bros., 1950), p. 45.

[2] *Ibid.,* pp. 51-53.

[3] *Ibid.,* pp. 74-76.

[4] *Ibid.,* p. 79.

[5] *Ibid.,* pp. 80-84.

[6] *Ibid.,* pp. 84-86.

[7] *Ibid.,* pp. 108-16.

[8] *Ibid.,* pp. 117-18.

## CHAPTER 7

[1] Louis Fischer, *op. cit.* Ch. 6, f.n. 1, p. 124.

[2] *Ibid.,* p. 134.

[3] *Ibid.,* p. 134.

[4] *Ibid.,* pp. 129-43.

[5] *Ibid.,* p. 176.

[6] *Ibid.,* p. 177.

[7] *Ibid.,* p. 179.

[8] *Ibid.,* pp. 181-84.

[9] *Ibid.,* p. 189.

[10] *Ibid.,* p. 194.

[11] *Ibid.,* p. 218.

[12] *Ibid.,* p. 244.

[13] *Ibid.,* p. 156.

[14] *Ibid.,* pp. 221-22.

[15] *Ibid.,* pp. 251-56.

[16] *Ibid.,* pp. 260-62.

[17] *Ibid.,* pp. 263-75.

[18] *Ibid.,* p. 275.

[19] *Ibid.,* p. 275.

[20] *Ibid.,* pp. 276, 278-79, 288.

[21] *Ibid.,* pp. 306-07.

[22] *Ibid.,* pp. 315-17.

[23] *Ibid.,* pp. 318-21.

[24] *Ibid.,* p. 320.

[25] *Ibid.,* p. 145.

[26] *Ibid.,* pp. 477-78, 494-502.

[27] *Ibid.,* Chapter I.

## Chapter 8

[1]Narayan Desai, *Towards a Non-violent Revolution* (Indian Press Pub. Litd., Varanasi, 1972). pp. 126-128.
[2]*Ibid.,* part 6.

## Chapter 9

[1] Louis Fischer, *op. cit.* Ch. 6, f.n. 1, p. 346.
[2] *Ibid.,* p. 348.
[3] Richard B. Gregg, *The Power of Non-Violence* (Fellowship Publications, 1959), pp. 30-35.
[4]Andre Trocme, *The Stages of Nonviolence* (Fellowship of Reconciliation, 1953), pp. 4-6.

## Chapter 10

[1] Martin Luther King, Jr., *op. cit.* Ch. 2, f.n. 5, p. 43.
[2] *Ibid.,* pp. 56-57.
[3] *Ibid.,* pp. 62-64.
[4] *Ibid.,* pp. 44-49.
[5] *Ibid.,* p. 76.
[6] *Ibid.,* p. 80.
[7] *Ibid.,* p. 85.
[8] *Ibid.,* p. 103.
[9] *Ibid.,* p. 122.
[10] *Ibid.,* p. 124.
[11] *Ibid.,* pp. 126-30.
[12] *Ibid.,* pp. 132-38.
[13] *Ibid.,* p. 140.
[14] *Ibid.,* p. 142.
[15] *Ibid.,* pp. 146-49.
[16] *Ibid.,* pp. 151-53.
[17] *Ibid.,* pp. 157-62.
[18] *Ibid.,* p. 175.
[19] *Ibid.,* pp. 163-65.
[20] *Ibid.,* pp. 174-80.
[21] *Ibid.,* p. 183.
[22] *Ibid.,* p. 180.
[23] *Ibid.,* p. 215.
[24]Howell Raines, *My Soul is Rested* (Bantam Books, N.Y., 1977), p. 79.
[25]James Peck, *Freedom Ride* (Grove Press, New York, N.Y., 1962).

## Chapter 11

[1] See p. 33.
[2] Louis Fischer, *op. cit.* Ch. 6, f.n. 1, p. 130.
[3] *Ibid.,* pp. 251-56.
[4] Martin Luther King, Jr., *op. cit.* Ch. 2, f.n. 5, pp. 164-69.

## Chapter 12

[1]Peter Matthiessen, *Sal Si Puedes: Cesar Chavez and the New American Revolution* (Random House, New York, 1969) p. 84
[2]Marjory Hope and James Young, *The Struggle for Humanity: Agents of Nonviolent Change in a Violent World* (Orbis Books, New York, N.Y., 1977) p. 163.
[3]*Ibid.,* p. 160.

## CHAPTER 13

[1] See pp. 6-9.

## CHAPTER 15

[1] Louis Fischer, *op. cit.* Ch. 6, f.n. 1, pp. 155-56.

## CHAPTER 16

[1] N. K. Bose, *op. cit.* Ch. 2, f.n. 4, Par. 446.

[2] Allan A. Hunter, *op. cit.* Ch. 1, f.n. 3, pp. 72-73.

[3] A. Ruth Fry, *op. cit.* Ch. 1, f.n. 2, pp. 52-53.

[4] Bradford Lyttle, *National Defense Thru Non-Violent Resistance* (Shahn-Ti Sena Publications, 5729 Dorchester Avenue, Chicago 37, Ill., 2d ed., 1959) Chapter IX.